MULESKINNER

THE EUROPEAN WAR
OF A NIAGARA ARTILLERYMAN

William Hesler

With extracts from *War Interlude*

by

Driver Harold Hesler

iUniverse, Inc.
Bloomington

Muleskinner
The European War of a Niagara Artilleryman

iUniverse books may be ordered through booksellers or by contacting:

iUniverse
1663 Liberty Drive
Bloomington, IN 47403
www.iuniverse.com
1-800-Authors (1-800-288-4677)

Because of the dynamic nature of the Internet, any Web addresses or links contained in this book may have changed since publication and may no longer be valid.

ISBN: 978-1-4502-7157-8 (sc)
ISBN: 978-1-4502-7158-5 (dj)
ISBN: 978-1-4502-7159-2 (ebk)

Printed in the United States of America

iUniverse rev. date: 11/30/2010

Note on the quotations

Quotations in plain typeface are from Harold Hesler's *War Interlude*. Those in italics are from other texts. Extracts from Divisional Ammunition Column War Diaries are framed.

311,972 Driver Harold Hesler,
No. 3 Section, 3ʳᵈ Divisional Ammunition Column

"I also had my photograph taken in Winnipeg which shows me as I felt."

INTRODUCTION

My father was born in 1893, in Humberstone, which is now part of Port Colborne, Ontario. Port Colborne is in the south-east corner of the Niagara Peninsula, about twenty miles west of Niagara Falls.

Harold Hesler was one of the 620,000 members of the Canadian Expeditionary Force in World War I. When asked later what he did in the war, he would reply simply that he was in the Artillery, and that he had been a muleskinner in France and Belgium.

The term "muleskinner" is rather misleading. My father spent the better part of the war on horseback. He was never that fond of horses, but he had a real affection for the mules that did most of the work in the Artillery. These worthy animals had a reputation for stubbornness which in turn bred the generally unfounded assumption that they had to be constantly whipped by their drivers. Thus was born the epithet which, although originally intended to malign both the animal and the man, ironically became a proud boast by the latter. What both had to go through in the course of World War I explains why.

My father never talked much about the war, or his experience in it, except for one or two anecdotes about the bizarre behaviour of officers, the stupidity of horses and how he had promoted himself from private to sergeant just weeks before his discharge. He told me he had written it all down, and that I could read it someday.

One out of every two Canadians who served at the front in France and Belgium during World War I was either killed or wounded. The impact on a whole generation of Canadians was staggering. By today's standards, it is practically impossible to understand how the social and political institutions of the day could have tolerated the slaughter.

The written record which my father left of his experience, entitled *"War Interlude"*, says little of the horrors to which he bore witness. He may have been waiting for someone else to put his personal account into context. This is what I have tried to do in this short study. For each of the events he experienced, I focus on the words he used in *"War Interlude"*, and then zoom out to a larger canvas recorded in the words of other participants, from private to field marshal, and from poet to prime minister. In some instances, I have reproduced entries in the official war diary kept by Driver Hesler's unit[1]. I have also tried to give the reader a taste of how different generations of historians have perceived the conflict and the role of Canadians in it.

The title *"War Interlude"* reflects the fact that the three-and-a-half-year stint that Harold Hesler did in the Canadian Army was the only period in his working life that he did not spend in the employ of the Royal Bank of Canada. He first joined the Bank as a junior clerk at Welland in 1910, at the age of 16. He resigned from the Winnipeg branch in January 1916 to enlist. A few weeks after being discharged from the Army, he rejoined the Royal Bank in Montreal in July, 1919. He did not leave the Bank again until his retirement in 1951.

Harold Hesler's banking career was a notable one. He was Secretary of the Bank and of its Board of Directors from 1934 to 1945. For many years he was in charge of all the Bank's foreign operations, a task rooted in the ten years he spent in Cuba after the war.

Harold Hesler's military career was noteworthy for one reason—he survived. Following his discharge in 1919 at the age of 25, he was refused life insurance because of his exposure to poison gas, but he lived until just before his eighty-ninth birthday.

The first illustration reproduced in *War Interlude* is an etching by the war artist Kerr Eby which appeared in the New York Times Magazine of November 10, 1940. It shows a team of muleskinners like my father, trying to advance through a muddy wasteland like the ones he lived in from 1916 to 1918. Under the drawing appear the words of the article's author, the American journalist and WWI vet Samuel Williamson:

"But in all the filth and stupidities of that experience I saw courage, fortitude, sacrifice."[2]

Under the clipping, my father has written simply:

"The words might almost be mine".

That seems to be as far as he wanted to go in expressing his true feelings about what he saw and heard.

W.H. August 14, 2010

CHAPTER ONE

PRELUDE TO THE INTERLUDE

The Big Picture

Palmer's *History of the Modern World* contains a succinct account of the circumstances leading up to the First World War. It reads like a board game. It is a story of intense rivalries between historic allies, hastily-fashioned alliances with old enemies, absurd posturing over matters *geopolitik* and an insane craving of a fight for the sake of the fight. On one side, the key allied players were the French, their ancient enemies the British, the Russians (previously at war with both the French and the British in the Crimea), and the Italians (historic foes of the French and allies of the Germans and Austrians only a few months before they joined the fray). On the other side, common cause was made by the Germans (who had been Britain's old ally against the French, and whose royal family was closely intertwined with Britain's), the Austro-Hungarians (likewise erstwhile friends of the British), and the Turks (centuries-old enemies of the Austro-Hungarians, and occasional collaborators with the French). Japan (which had recently beaten the Russians), was a peripheral ally of the British, but only to the extent dictated by its ambitions in East Asia. Sitting on the sidelines for most of the war were the Americans. Other, less important players, joined in at one point or another, with a keen eye to which side was winning, such as tiny Honduras, which declared war on the German Empire four months before the end. A few profited from neutrality (notably the Swedes, the Danes, the Dutch, the Spanish and the Swiss). Some countries, like Belgium, were trampled in the rush to stake out a position on the board.

Until 1914, Europe had been spared a major conflagration for practically a century. Since the fall of Napoleon, there had been wars, but they were short and snappy affairs fought by relatively small armies. By the dawn of the twentieth century, industrialization had created the resources, both human and material, for confrontations on a much larger scale. The Americans had shown the way with a bloody war of attrition in 1860-65 that in some respects was a model for what was to take place in Europe from 1914 to 1918. Instead of the battles of the 17th and 18th Centuries in which contingents of mercenaries would duel each other to settle a quarrel between their retainers, the new model called for thousands of conscripts to throw their bodies against the firepower of the enemy until one side or the other ran out of bodies.

The surplus population and social organization of the European powers made it possible by 1914 to stage battles in which not just thousands, but hundreds of thousands of men would hurl themselves upon the enemy. By that time, however, developments in the science of artillery and the invention of the machine gun enabled the enemy to cope. On July 1, 1916, two weeks before Driver Hesler landed in France, the British Army lost 57,470 men killed and wounded in a single day of the Battle of the Somme.

It is difficult to grasp what it was that made people submit to this kind of sacrifice and what was going through the minds of the men who sent them to the slaughter. Revulsion at the loss of human life must have been well suppressed, for the following year the forces of the British Empire suffered 280,000 casualties[1] at Passchendaele. 15,654 were Canadians.

The Second World War erupted out of the determination of Germany and Japan (and to some extent Russia) to aggress their neighbours, to destroy or confiscate their homes and means of livelihood, and to enslave or simply kill them. It was an event characterized by evil. In the First World War, territorial designs were secondary and the civilian populations were largely spared except for famine and disease. It was a war characterized by stupidity. The politicians and diplomats who allowed it to happen did not seem to understand what was happening. The generals who conducted the war were seemingly oblivious to the sacrifice in human lives that their orders routinely required. It was not the oppression of one people by another. It was a war in which each side preyed upon itself.

Like its American model of 1860-65, it was a war that everyone expected would be over in a couple of months. It lasted more than four years. When it ended, it was not immediately apparent who, if anyone, had won. There was no surrender, just an armistice. At the outset and for most of the war, there was no clear enunciation by either side of the purpose for which it was fighting. One author described the "prime heresy" of the war as being the almost universally held conviction "that determination can do the work of intelligence":

> *"That this illusion could persist so long and so strongly at general headquarters on both sides is a certain indication that the men in control of the War knew almost nothing about its realities. They thought in abstract terms, while war works concretely upon vulnerable flesh and blood. . . . They failed to realize that war is a machine which enslaves those who set it going, as well as millions innocent of any professional interest in it."* [2]

When it was over, the male populations of the participating countries had been bled white. 8,500,000 had been killed and another 21,000,000 wounded. More than a third of the casualties occurred in an area of a few hundred square miles in northern France and Flanders. This is the area in which Harold Hesler moved about on foot and on horseback for nearly three years and which is described by him in his *"War Interlude"*.

The Geography

Driver Hesler's World War I odyssey took him by train from Winnipeg to St. John, New Brunswick, and then by ship to Liverpool, via Halifax. By the time he landed in France on July 15, 1916, he had travelled nearly 7,000 miles. He and his unit of the 3rd Divisional Artillery then moved another 120 miles by train from the port of Le Havre to a camp near a village called Godewaersvelde, about a mile from the Belgian border.

3

Except for three brief trips on leave to Paris and Britain, he would spend the next two and a half years in an area measuring about 60 miles from north to south, and 30 miles wide. The northeast corner of this territory is the Belgian village of Passchendaele. Along the southern flank is the River Somme. Roughly in the middle is Vimy Ridge. These three points mark the major Canadian engagements in which he participated prior to the Allied breakthrough in the last hundred days of the war. After 1915, this was generally the area assigned to the British forces, including the colonial and "Dominion" contingents. To the south of them were the French.

After the rapid initial German advance on Paris in 1914 had been repulsed in September at the first battle of the Marne, the war ceased to be a war of movement. It became a trench-bound war of attrition along a line that stretched from the Belgian North Sea coast to the Swiss border. In the north, where most of the fighting took place, the line between the Germans on one side and the British and French on the other formed a sort of crescent that started at a point on the Belgian coast about 20 miles east of Dunkirk. From there, it ran southwards to a point about 50 miles northeast of Paris and then curved towards the east and Verdun. Between November 1914 and July 1918, this line shifted back and forth throughout its length, but never by more than 23 miles. Some of the places where Driver Hesler and his unit encamped in 1916 and 1917 were overrun by the Germans in their last offensive during the spring of 1918.

The French make extremely good road maps, which manage to show with extraordinary clarity the innumerable towns, villages and hamlets that dot their countryside. On Michelin's map of *France - Nord*, there are about seventy place names mentioned by Harold Hesler in *War Interlude*. Some of these ceased to exist while he was there, and have been rebuilt. The map shows in clear detail the web of little country roads that fan out from either side of the *Autoroute du Nord (A-1)* and the *A-26*. There is scarcely a strand of the web that does not show a foreign military cemetery. Most are marked with a *"Brit."*, but some have a *"Cdn."*. Even now, few roadmaps can evoke the feelings that this one does.

LA CARTE DU THEATRE DE LA GUERRE

MAP OF THE EASTERN AND WESTERN FRONTS FROM A GERMAN PROPAGANDA BOOKLET "LIBERATED" BY DRIVER HESLER AT VALENCIENNES, NOVEMBER 3, 1918[3]

The Military "Science"

The situation in which the opposing forces found themselves at the end of 1914 called for new methods of war. As the French had learned in August when they attempted to counterattack the Germans in Lorraine, the machine gun made the ordinary massed infantry attack suicidal. The establishment of a line of trenches from the North Sea to Switzerland practically eliminated the traditional alternative of outflanking the enemy.

The new theory of warfare was based on artillery. The idea was that massive artillery bombardment would destroy the enemy's barbed wire, his trenches and enough of his men, with the result that the infantry could then advance without excessive casualties. The new theory was put to the test on a grand scale. It is estimated that a total of 170,385,295 artillery shells were expended by the British forces alone in the course of the war[4]. At the Battle of the Somme, the British lobbed a total of 3,526,000 artillery rounds at the Germans in two weeks. By way of comparison, it is estimated that Napoleon had about 20,000 rounds for his guns at Waterloo[5].

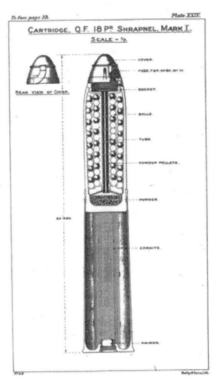

TECHNICAL DRAWING OF AN 18-POUNDER SHRAPNEL SHELL FROM THE FIELD MANUAL CARRIED BY DRIVER HESLER

The new method failed, however, to produce the intended result. Every barrage became a signal to the enemy that an attack was imminent and a beacon pinpointing where it would occur. The terrain became so devastated by successive barrages that the attackers had difficulty advancing over it before the defenders could reposition their machine guns. So much effort had to be expended to achieve anything that it was practically impossible to gain more than a few hundred yards at a time. Whatever ground was captured usually was taken at greater cost to the attackers than the toll levied on the enemy. Successful attackers who penetrated the line to any significant extent soon became defenders on three sides instead of one.

The new warfare might at first appear as a contest between opposing masses of infantry, but in many respects it was a test of the ability of the infantry on both sides to survive in the abattoir of the combined artillery. Two-thirds of the casualties in the war were inflicted by artillery. Front-line infantrymen were exposed at irregular intervals to rifle and machine gun fire, exploding grenades and poison gas, but everyone on the ground was constantly exposed to the shelling.

> *"Shell wounds were the most to be feared, because of the multiple effects shell explosion could produce in the human body. At its worst it could disintegrate a human being, so that nothing recognizable—sometimes apparently nothing at all—remained of him . . . Less spectacular, but sometimes as deadly, shell blast could create over-pressures or vacuums in the body's organs, rupturing the lungs and producing haemorrhages in the brain and spinal cord . . . Much the most common wounding by shell fire, however, was by splinter or shrapnel ball."* [6]

Tremendous industrial and physical effort was invested in producing this carnage. Driver Hesler was the second-to-last link in a chain which began in the munitions factories[7] and ended with the gunner who pulled the firing lanyard on the gun. He was part of a Divisional Ammunition Column, a mounted unit whose mission was to bring ammunition from the railhead supply dumps to the guns of the Canadian Artillery. In ideal conditions this was done with wagons pulled by horses or mules, sometimes over narrow-gauge rail lines. Conditions were usually such that the rail lines were knocked out by the enemy's artillery and the wagons could not be moved through the mud. The ammunition had to be strapped over the backs of the animals, while the drivers coaxed them forward on foot. Occasionally, as at Passchendaele, the drivers became the mules. During the major engagements, with their barrages lasting several days, the route to the guns was blanketed by German counter-artillery. In quieter periods, sporadic shelling was a constant harassment to any form of movement near the lines. While Driver Hesler never had to dread being called up "over the top" of a trench, to march forward unprotected against machine gun fire, his duties required him to move almost daily over open ground exposed to exploding shells. They all missed him, but many of the men he worked with were not so lucky. We can only wonder what it did to him to see men he knew blown apart or writhing in agony. Not once in his *War Interlude* does he mention seeing anyone killed or wounded, and he never refers to the bloodbaths he witnessed beyond a perfunctory mention that "casualties were heavy".

CHAPTER TWO

THE WAR UP TO JULY 1916

The worst was yet to come, but much had occurred in the war before Driver Hesler arrived in France.

The Germans invaded Belgium on August 4, 1914 and were within 20 miles of the Eiffel Tower a month later. Over-extended and caught off guard by the orderliness of the British and French withdrawal, the Germans were repulsed at the first battle of the Marne and withdrew in turn. Canada, still little more than a self-governing colony of the British Empire, had found itself at war the instant Great Britain entered it. When the First Canadian Contingent left Quebec City on October 1, the conflict was moving into a deadlock along a line that would scarcely move until 1918. The first two months of the war had been fast, thick and furious. In the three weeks from August 21 to September 12, the French alone suffered more than 600,000 casualties. However, if anyone thought that the change from a war of movement to a stalemate would improve matters in terms of casualties, they were mistaken.

The 31,200 hastily-assembled Canadians who sailed from Quebec City in a flotilla of 32 ships were the largest military force up until then to cross the Atlantic in one movement, and the first to do so under threat of submarine attack. After four months of training in appalling winter conditions in makeshift facilities in southern England, the 20,000 troops of the 1st Canadian Division landed in France in February, 1915. Between March 10 and 12, they played a minor role at Neuve Chapelle, the first major battle resulting from a British attempt to break the deadlock. This inconclusive engagement produced 25,000 casualties, only a few of them Canadian. It is doubtful that the Canadians were fully aware that three days of battle had reduced the Imperial ranks by a number greater than their own total fighting strength.

The Canadian involvement began in earnest in April, shortly after the 1st Division was moved north as part of the British Second Army, to relieve part of the French forces around Ypres. Ypres was the focal point of a large Allied protrusion into German-held territory. This ancient medieval Belgian town had already been the site of one major battle the previous November. Heavily damaged by German bombardment but still functioning, it would be virtually destroyed by the end of the war.[1]

Like the pioneers that many of them had been at home, the Canadians immediately went about improving the defensive positions left behind by the French in the portion of this salient north-east of the town. Their efforts were hampered by the high water table and the fact that the ground was littered with dead, buried and unburied.

On April 22, the Germans launched an offensive which began the Second Battle of Ypres. Prior to the attack, the Germans had installed 5,700 cylinders of chlorine gas in the ground in front of their lines, and they opened the valves when the easterly wind was strong enough to carry the gas over the French and Canadian positions in front of the village of St. Julien. Intelligence reports of what the Germans were up to were dismissed by the British and French high commands as unworthy of belief, probably because the Geneva Convention "outlawed" the use of poison gas. No protective measures of any sort were made available to the troops. A quick-thinking medical officer[2] from Montreal's Royal Victoria Hospital recognized the smell of the gas. Knowing that chlorine will crystallize if exposed to ammonia, he spread the word for the men to urinate into whatever bit of cloth they could find and hold the improvised filter to their faces. Those who did were among the lucky survivors who were then faced with having to defend themselves against the rifles and grenades of the advancing German infantry.

The French line broke in complete disarray, but the Canadian line held and moved in to cover the gap left by the French. To make matters worse, the Canadians found that their Ross rifles jammed from the heat of rapid firing. A second wave of gas hit them two days later, but they continued to hold and even managed to mount a counter-attack out of the chaos. The brigade which took the brunt of the action was led by Arthur Currie, a part-time soldier from Victoria, B.C., about whom much more will be said before this story is over[3].

It is difficult to imagine the horror and suffering endured by the Canadians who were hit by these first gas attacks. For some, the injury was comparatively light. For several hundred, the inhalation of the chlorine gas led to a slow death by gradual asphyxiation over a period of days:

> *"There, sitting on the bed, fighting for breath, his lips plum-coloured, his hue leaden, was a magnificent young Canadian past all hope in the asphyxia of chlorine . . . I shall never forget the look in his eyes as he turned to me and gasped: 'I can't die! Is it possible that nothing can be done for me?'"* [4]

An intense series of German thrusts and Allied counter-attacks lasted throughout the Ypres salient until the end of May. Aided by superior numbers, effective artillery and repeated gas attacks, the Germans succeeded in pushing the line back towards the town, but they failed to achieve a breakthrough.

The stand made by the Canadians during the first three days of utter confusion was credited by the British War Office as having "undoubtedly saved the situation". Ferdinand Foch, the French field-marshal who later assumed overall command of the Allied forces, is reported as having said that it "was the finest act of the War". But generals are fond of praising determined acts of fortitude in the face of impending disaster.

Some Canadian units were decimated. One regiment with a particularly quaint name—Princess Patricia's Canadian Light Infantry[5]—began at Ypres a history of horrific battlefield encounters which was to continue on through two world wars, Korea and Afghanistan. On May 8, it lost 392 men in a single day holding off repeated German assaults on the ridge above the village of Frezenberg. By the time they were relieved, the P.P.C.L.I. were down to a strength of four officers and 150 men, where before the battle they had been 1,000.

Ypres II cost 6,500 Canadian casualties. It inspired another Canadian front-line medical officer, John McCrae[6], to write what is said to be the best-known poem of the First World War:

In Flanders fields the poppies blow
Between the crosses, row on row,
That mark our place; and in the sky
The larks, still bravely singing, fly
Scarce heard amid the guns below.

We are the Dead. Short days ago
We lived, felt dawn, saw sunset glow,
Loved and were loved, and now we lie,
In Flanders fields.

Meanwhile the French had embarked on a costly and futile offensive to the south, in the Artois region west of Vimy Ridge. The French commander-in-chief, General Joffre, accusing the British of not pulling their weight, goaded the British commander, General French, into supporting the offensive in that sector. As a result, the 1st Canadian Division was transferred from the British Second Army at Ypres southwards to General Haig's First Army near where the Division had first seen action at Neuve Chapelle. Only two weeks after losing half their fighting strength at Ypres, the Canadians were ordered into a series of inconclusive attacks on German positions heavily defended by artillery and machine guns near the villages of Festubert and Givenchy. The experience at Festubert (May 15-25), at a cost of 2,500 Canadian casualties, was a demonstration of the confusion and poor co-ordination that could result from being slotted into a patchwork of British units with shifting command responsibilities. Givenchy (June 15) was scarcely more successful, but showed that the Canadians were learning from past mistakes and assuming greater initiative in matters of planning and artillery support.

When the French gave up their Artois assault, the British resumed a passive defensive role. On June 24, the 1st Canadian Division was moved northward to rejoin the Second Army near Armentières, and from then until mid-September enjoyed a period of relative calm along its sector of the line. The summer was spent integrating reinforcements and developing techniques of attack and defence based on the recent experiences.

One of these techniques was the use of indirect machine gun fire, in addition to artillery, in support of the infantry. The idea of supporting the infantry with friendly machine gun fire over their heads from the rear was rejected by the British and the French, until the methods for doing so safely and effectively were developed and demonstrated by a rather remarkable individual named Raymond Brutinel. A French immigrant to Western Canada, Brutinel was a millionaire and living in Montreal when the war broke out. With his own money and contributions from people like Sir Herbert Holt, president of the Royal Bank of Canada, he raised the 1st Canadian Motor Machine Gun Brigade. Brutinel had been a captain in the French Army before his arrival in Canada, and his decision not to resume his French commission at the outbreak of war probably saved a lot of Canadian lives. By the end of the war he was a Brigadier-General in command of the Canadian Machine Gun Corps.

Meanwhile, the 2nd Canadian Division had been assembled in Canada, shipped to England and arrived in the Hazebrouk area southeast of Ypres by September 21. The arrival of the 2nd Division marked the formation of the Canadian Corps[7], to be joined the following spring by the 3rd Division, and later in 1916, by the 4th Division. The establishment of a corps command enabled the Canadians to assume a more distinct identity as a fighting force, which in turn led to a greater degree of influence in the tactical decisions affecting the men in the line. By the end of the war, the Canadian Corps would become the most effective fighting unit on the Allied side.

This expansion of the Canadian forces coincided with concerted efforts by the Canadian Government to oppose the appointment of British officers to senior positions of command. In one of the early salvos of a bloodless colonial revolution, Prime Minister Borden instructed the Canadian High Commissioner[8] in London as follows:

> *"Apparently there is some movement by the British professional soldiers, or officials of the War Office and British Staff Officers to supersede Canadians in the higher commands of our troops. . . . You may tell [Colonial*

> *Secretary] Mr. Bonar Law, Lord Kitchener [Secretary of*
> *State for War] and [Prime Minister] Mr. Asquith for me*
> *that we will not permit anything of the kind."* [9]

Departing from the practice which prompted these urgings, the British had already decided to promote the Canadian, Arthur Currie to the rank of Major-General and put him in command of the 1st Division. At 39, he was one of the youngest to hold that rank in the British and Dominion forces, and the first non-regular officer to do so.

At the end of September, the British embarked on another offensive, again at the insistence of the French, who had decided to renew their Artois campaign. The British effort, known as the Battle of Loos, was even more costly than Ypres II had been and accomplished nothing. It was a kind of deliberate sacrifice undertaken to assist the French, despite the knowledge that the British would not have sufficient artillery and ammunition to support another major offensive until the following year. The French themselves gained little. They reached the crest of Vimy Ridge, but were driven back. British casualties were 60,000. The French lost 200,000. Fortunately, the Canadian involvement was insignificant. The main consequence of the bungled battle for the Canadians was a change in the British command, with General French being replaced by General Haig as Commander-in-Chief. It was not a fortuitous decision. By the end of the war, Haig would come to epitomize the insensitivity and stupidity which characterized the conflict as a whole.

As 1915 drew to a close, the outlook was bleak. On the Western Front, the war of attrition was costing the French and British about two casualties for every one German casualty. Winston Churchill's naval and land assault against the German-led Turks in the Dardanelles had been a disaster. The German and Austrians had inflicted appalling losses on the Russians, and the Eastern front had been pushed back as much as 300 miles.

It was against this background that Harold Hesler resigned from the Winnipeg branch of the Royal Bank of Canada and, on January 20, 1916, became a member of No. 3 Section, 3rd Divisional Ammunition Column. He was 22 years old. For the duration of the conflict, he would hold the rank of Driver, which was the equivalent of Gunner or Private.

"On March 6th we said good-bye to Winnipeg. I had been there such a short time that there was little cause for regret at leaving but a very deep regret that our leaving was arranged so quickly that I could not go home to say good-bye to my family.

A large proportion of our men came from farms on the prairies but Winnipeg was well represented so there was quite a rousing farewell for all of us. I can say that with few exceptions it was a congenial group of men.

Next afternoon we came to Fort William and were lined up on the station platform for inspection. I was refused permission to break ranks and speak to a dear friend who had come to the station to wish me luck."

The shortest rail line from Winnipeg to the port of St. John cut across the State of Maine, but Driver Hesler's troop train had to respect the neutrality of the United States and take the long way around, down the St. Lawrence and across the Gaspé Peninsula. After sailing from St. John to Halifax, he and his unit boarded the *S.S. Lapland*, part of a small convoy under the escort of a British cruiser.

"On March 21st the *Carnarvon* left us and we were taken over by another cruiser. On the 24th we enjoyed the sight of several destroyers ploughing towards us through the heavy seas. At times it seemed that they had been swamped but they eventually took us into their care and the cruiser went about other business. At about the same time we sighted land which must have been the west coast of Ireland and we were ordered to put on life belts which we wore until we pulled into the Mersey River next afternoon. The U-boat menace was ever-present but not as intense as it would be within a year."

The *Lapland* reached Liverpool on March 25. From March 27 to July 14, Driver Hesler trained with his unit in camps in Southern

England. While he was getting used to military life, things on the Continent were heating up.

During the winter of 1915-1916 the British forces engaged in a new policy of attempting to wear down the enemy with continuous sniping, trench raids and random artillery shoots. The Canadians became particularly skilful in nocturnal trench raiding methods, giving rise to the rumour amongst the Germans that the Canadian forces included significant numbers of what they called "Red Indians". In fact, the percentage of voluntary enlistment from amongst First Nation peoples was higher than from any other group in Canada. More than 3,500 chose life in the Army over life on the reserves.

Trench warfare took on another dimension in the spring, as each side expended enormous efforts, and vast amounts of explosives, tunnelling under each other's trenches and trying to blow them up. On March 27, one such operation by the British five miles south of Ypres near the village of St. Eloi produced a string of gigantic, sodden craters which battalions of the 2nd Canadian Division were then called upon to hold against German counter-attacks and heavy artillery bombardment. The operation turned into a fiasco when communications broke down and craters recaptured by Germans were mistaken for craters still held by Canadians. In addition to the lesson on communications, the St. Eloi craters taught the Canadians to be wary of trying to take and hold limited, static objectives which would then become the focus of the enemy's concentrated shell fire.

The fallout from the St. Eloi craters included a change in command of the Canadian Corps, and the appointment of Lieutenant-General Sir Julian Byng as Corps Commander. Like his predecessor Alderson, Byng was a British officer, but there was apparently no suggestion at the time that any of the Canadian generals was ready to fill the top position. That would not happen until the following year, when the commander of the 1st Division, Arthur Currie, took over a Corps which by then had doubled in size. It was under Byng, however, that the Canadian Corps attained a standing closer to that of an allied national force in its own right, as opposed to a mere colonial unit in the British Army. Byng was immensely popular with the Canadians[10].

At the beginning of June 1916, the Canadian Corps were holding the most easterly projection into German territory of the Ypres Salient. On

June 2, after extensive preparations and a devastating artillery barrage, the Germans over-ran the Canadian positions at Sanctuary Wood and Mount Sorrel. The commander of the 3rd Division, General Mercer, was killed. A replenished P.P.C.L.I. took 400 casualties, including its Colonel. Remnants of the Canadian trenches were mopped up with flame-throwers. It was the only occasion in the war when Canadian artillery pieces fell into German hands. A German regimental historian wrote of the engagement that: "It is fitting to stress that here too the Canadians did not surrender, but at their guns defended themselves with revolvers to the last man"[11]. The German advance might have been more successful had it not been for Brutinel, who disobeyed orders and moved his Motor Machine Gun Brigade out of reserve to cover the gap in the line.

Ten days later, the Canadians turned the tables. It was the first deliberately-planned attack ever executed by a Canadian force, and the planning made it an unqualified success. After bringing every available artillery resource to bear on the Germans, Currie's 1st Division needed only an hour to drive them back to their original lines. Two German counter-attacks failed, and the sector again settled into a stalemate with the two sides dug in less than 200 yards away from each other. In twelve days, the fighting at Sanctuary Wood and Mount Sorrel had consumed 8,000 Canadian casualties.

During this same period, a war of words that had gone on for over a year finally came to an end. The conflict involved the Canadian Ross rifle, and raged between the vast majority of the members of the Canadian Infantry on one hand, and Canada's egomaniacal Minister of Militia and Defence, Sir Samuel Hughes.

Hughes had gained some notoriety earlier in life when he recommended himself for a Victoria Cross for his participation in the South African War. Never daunted, he saw to it as Minister of Defence that he be given the highest military rank ever held up till then by a Canadian, Lieutenant-General[12]. Hughes even suggested that he be put in command of the Canadian Corps when it was formed.

The same Ross rifle which is a landmark in Quebec jurisprudence on manufacturer's liability[13] was the weapon initially issued to Canadian troops. The Ross was vigorously championed by Hughes, partly out of national pride and partly because he was a friend of Sir Charles Ross. At the ordeal of Ypres II, Canadian infantry started discarding the Ross and equipping themselves with the Lee-Enfields of dead British soldiers. By the time of the battles of Festubert and Givenchy, most of the 1st Division carried contraband Lee-Enfields. June 1916 marked the point at which the Canadian infantry were finally (and officially) relieved of their infamous Ross rifles. Hughes himself was the next to go. Procurement scandals, administrative excesses and his own pretentiousness were his undoing. His downfall began the same day that Driver Hesler laid eyes on him during an inspection of the 3rd Division in Southern England:

"On Tuesday, March 28th, we marched many muddy miles to be inspected by the controversial Sir Sam Hughes, Minister of Militia and Defence. Ironically on that same day in Parliament at Ottawa, Sir Sam's administration of his department was being strongly criticized, giving rise to the appointment of a Royal Commission which exonerated him but he was on the way out. His resignation was called for on November 14th and the department was divided between a representative in London and another in Ottawa."

A BREAK DURING BOOT CAMP AT WITLEY, SURREY, JUNE 1916
(DRIVER HESLER IS 3RD FROM LEFT, REAR ROW)

Driver Hesler's unit landed in France on July 15 and encamped first at Steenvoorde, then at Poperinghe, ten miles west of Ypres. During this period, with the focus of battle shifting south to the Somme, the role of the Canadian Corps around Ypres was "stationary yet aggressive", meaning sporadic artillery bombardment and trench raiding. From July 24 to August 24, Driver Hesler had his first experiences of night-time trips to the gun positions. From September 6 to October 2, his unit moved to a point near Kemmel, at the southern base of the Ypres Salient. Here he made his first trips directly to the front line in support of the trench mortars. From this position the Canadians were still shelling the Germans around the St. Eloi craters.

WAR DIARY OF THE 3RD DIVISIONAL AMMUNITION COLUMN FOR
AUGUST 9, 1916:

Gas attack. Horses & mules affected—one dying—2 had to be shot. 6 men sent to hospital gassed. Men now have confidence in gas helmets. One man killed, stray bullet.

"We had been issued with gas-masks, the grey Ku Klux Klan model, which had come into use in November 1915 following the improvised protectors used after the Second Battle of Ypres. It fitted into a small bag carried on a shoulder sling. Later in the year these were replaced by the box respirator. Steel helmets had been brought into use in late 1915 but distribution was slow and we did not receive our full supply until after several weeks. In the meantime the supply was pooled and drawn on by those 'going up the line'. Weighing about two pounds there was always a temptation to shed them but anyone caught doing so was severely reprimanded. Our move to the front also coincided with the withdrawal of the Ross rifle and the substitution of the Lee Enfield with which our complement of about fifty was filled."

Although the 3rd Division infantry moved out of the Ypres area in August, the 3rd Divisional Artillery stayed on in this role until October 3. On that day, it began a week-long trek to the Somme.

"At the overnight stops shelter for the men was sometimes improvised by slanting a tarpaulin over a support to accommodate six or eight men but in the rear areas a barn or other building was often available. Sunny France at this time of year was far from bright weather-wise and if we could be glad at all we were glad that we were in a mounted unit as each driver had two saddle blankets which could be used for greater warmth by a driver, as I was, or shared with a non-driver, the latter category making up about one-third of the establishment. As an added benefit it was claimed that saddle blankets which had been on horses or mules were lice repellents but in my experience, which began soon after we arrived on the continent, that was a myth."

CHAPTER THREE

THE SOMME

Driver Hesler's unit of the 3rd Divisional Artillery saw action in the latter part of what became known as the Battle of the Somme.

Many of the engagements of the war that were given battle names were not battles in the traditional sense, but rather prolonged sieges. Unlike the siege of a fortress or a town, the siege of a trench system gave a distinct advantage to the besieged. Instead of being cut off and attacked from all sides, the defenders' routes of supply to the rear usually remained open. If overrun, they only needed to retreat a few hundred yards to another line of trenches, and the siege would either begin all over again, or the attackers would become the besieged. Stretched out over miles of open ground, these engagements consumed unprecedented numbers of combatants on both sides.

The most costly such "battle" of the war was the series of assaults on the German fortified trench system in northern France along the high ground which forms the watershed between the River Somme and its tributary, the River Ancre. Before 1916, the British line ended and the French line began near Arras, a town located about 20 miles north of the triangle formed by the Ancre and the Somme. Early in 1916, the British relieved the northern end of the French line almost as far as the Somme. At that point, the French forces had practically exhausted themselves, having endured the brunt of the German attacks. The most recent of these was the siege of Verdun. At Verdun, territorial objectives had been ranked second by the Germans. Their main strategy was directed at killing and maiming as many Frenchmen as possible. From February to June 1916 they succeeded in doing so to over 300,000 of them. In the mind of the German chief of staff, von Falkenhayn, the British were "the arch-enemy in this war", and the plan to bleed the French forces to death was designed to deprive Britain of her "best sword".

In June 1916, the focus of conflict shifted from the French lines to the British. From then until the end of the war, the decisive battles on the Western Front would be fought along the line which separated the British and German armies.

In December, 1915, the politicians and generals of France, Britain, Russia and Italy had agreed that each of their nations would launch a major offensive against the Germans and Austrians during the following summer. The British Commander-in-Chief, General Sir Douglas Haig, would have preferred to attack along the northern end of his line near Ypres.

Haig was a dour, inarticulate Scot of the same wealthy family who owned the distillery of that name. Fit and good-looking, Haig was well-positioned in the British power establishment, and was a protégé of King George V. He often wrote in his diary that his plans were guided by the hand of God. He began the war already convinced that tactics of attrition were the way of the future.

The Ypres area was already familiar ground to Haig. It was also the burial ground for tens of thousands of his men. Tens of thousands more would join them there in 1917 during the Battle of Passchendaele. In the interim, it was at the southern end of the British line, just north of the Somme and seventy miles north of Paris, that Haig was instructed to attack.

The ground held by the Germans astride the Somme had some tactical value, but there was no real strategic advantage to be gained by Haig's campaign as a whole. The original plan was to take the Germans by surprise and begin the attack after a brief but intense artillery bombardment, with the infantry advancing in semi-darkness before dawn. The Germans, on the other hand, had known for weeks that an attack was coming. The preparations were carried out so openly that the British Prime Minister, Lloyd George later likened them to "an old Chancery suit, where the most detailed pleadings informed the defendant to the minutest particular of every point that would have to be met and fought out"[1]. In addition, in order to coordinate with a French advance to the south, the British artillery bombardment was stretched out over seven days. It was not until 48 hours after it had begun to fall off for lack of ammunition that the signal was given for the infantry to move. The attack was then launched in broad daylight on the morning of July 1, by which time the German machine gunners had emerged from the safety of their dug-outs.

The unprecedented number of shells which had been raining down on the German positions for days had relatively little effect. Most of them were from 18-pounder guns which had no effect at all on German dugouts thirty feet below the surface. Worse still, the shells used were of the shrapnel type, so deadly against men and animals in the open, but nearly useless in the effort to cut and flatten the enemy's barbed wire.

Along a front 14 miles long, spread out in single lines abreast, the British infantry were ordered to advance towards the enemy trenches at a slow walk. The cessation of artillery fire was the signal for the start of a forlorn and hopeless race in which the heavily-laden attackers would have to cover several hundred yards in less time than it would take the German machine gunners to climb the thirty feet of ladder from their dugouts to the parapets of their firing positions.

It must have become fairly obvious early in the day that the assumptions regarding the effect of the artillery had been disastrously wrong. The British field commanders who could have halted the attack probably then assumed that enough of their troops would remain untouched by the raking machine gun fire to be able to reach the German trenches and then engage in hand-to-hand combat and kill or drive out the German soldiers who were firing at them. The British tactical training manuals, drawn up for colonial wars in the days of the single shot rifle, contained tables showing that successive waves of attack would in the end overwhelm a defending infantry force. The machine gun slaughter of tens of thousands of Frenchmen in the first months of the war had already proved that this theory no longer applied. The Battle of the Somme showed just how wrong it could be.

On the first day, out of the advancing lines of British troops, 57,470 were mowed down, 21,000 of them fatally. The 1st Newfoundland Regiment was virtually annihilated. In many cases, the attackers became entangled in barbed wire and could not even turn back or take cover. In one truly bizarre instance, four battalions of British troops were pointlessly sent off to be massacred as they marched forward over a mile of open ground *behind* their own front line.

One wonders what must have gone through the minds of the German machine gunners. Initially, the sudden appearance in the distance of so many advancing men must have struck terrible fear in them. As successive waves of these slow-moving attackers crumpled into the mud, fear must have given away to relief, then disbelief and later, disgust:

> *"We were very surprised to see them walking, we had never seen that before . . . The officers went in front. I noticed one of them walking calmly, carrying a walking stick. When we started firing we just had to load and reload. They went down in their hundreds. You didn't have to aim, we just fired into them."*[2]

The most incredible thing about the first day of the battle of the Somme was that it did not prevent the continuation of the same sort of suicidal frontal assault, under deteriorating conditions, relentlessly over the next five months. By the time it was over, the Allied forces had lost more than 600,000 killed and wounded. Not jaded by their successes at Verdun, the Germans had their own name for the Battle of the Somme: *der Blutbad*.

The Canadians were kept out of it until September.

ARTILLERYMEN AT ORVILLE, OCTOBER 1916
FOREGROUND, LEFT TO RIGHT: DRIVERS FARTHERING, PARKINSON, HESLER,
PATTERSON, LEGG AND RUMBAUGH
MAN IN REAR IN DARK SWEATER: SGT. GEORGE WILSON

Driver Hesler and his unit of the 3rd Divisional Artillery did not arrive in the Somme area until October 7, 1916. Quebec's 22nd Battalion (later to become the *Royal 22ième Régiment*) had taken the village of Courcelette on September 15. The Vandoos' lieutenant-colonel wrote that "If hell is as bad as what I have seen at Courcelette, I would not wish my worst enemy to go there"[3]. Hesler writes:

> "When we reached the Somme area a month later Courcelette and Martinpuich, separated by the Albert-Bapaume road, were not distinguishable as villages in the sea of mud which had been churned up in the rainy fall weather which ensued."

On October 10, near Aveluy, Driver Hesler passed by the wrecks of the tanks which, a month earlier, had been the first ever used in war:

> "Here for the first time we saw some of the tanks that had been too hastily introduced into battle in September and were now lying derelict."

The living conditions which greeted Canadian soldiers arriving at the front were as bad as they would ever be:

> *"Sanitation, of course, was primitive. Lice soon fed on the bodies of the living, rats on the bodies of the dead. Clothing became impregnated with the slimy, foul-smelling mud, and the stench of death and latrines was so prevalent that only the newcomers noticed it."* [4]

Two miles north-west of Courcelette the Germans held a defensive position known as Regina Trench. This was the objective assigned to the 1st and 3rd Canadian Divisions in an episode of the Somme known as the Battle of Ancre Heights. Two costly assaults on the trench were attempted on October 1 and 8. They failed mainly because of the failure of the artillery to destroy the barbed wire entanglements which protected the trench. The newly-arrived Canadian 4th Division, supported by the combined strength of the 1st, 2nd and 3rd Divisional Artillery, took over the task.

> WAR DIARY OF THE 3ʳᵈ DIVISIONAL AMMUNITION COLUMN FOR OCTOBER 23, 1916:
>
> Dull & cold. Rain during night—Horse lines are now a quagmire, mud everywhere over foot deep. Sections all employed during day and night as working parties and carrying ammunition to battery gun positions. No 2 Section carried 610 rounds to 11ᵗʰ Brigade gun positions by means of strapping 4 ammunition baskets on each side of saddle as shell holes & roads too bad otherwise.

The early part of the Artillery's effort was not appreciated. One infantry battalion lost 200 men during an assault on October 21. An artillery observer admitted that the barrage was "absolutely insufficient to keep down enemy machine gun fire, there being not enough guns on the zone and the rate of fire was too slow"[5].

IMPROVISED SLINGS FOR THE MUD OF THE SOMME

The recriminations must have been taken to heart. Driver Hesler writes that from October 21 to November 18, "we were 'up the line' every night and sometimes during the daytime".

> "At first we made a few trips to the gun positions in the orthodox manner with limbered ammunition wagons drawn by six horses but the ground was becoming more churned up each day by enemy shelling and frequent and heavy rains. I recall an occasion when we had

twelve horses hitched to a wagon but could not drag it through the mud even when unlimbered and with men at the wheels. We improvised slings and packed the ammunition on the backs of the horses to the guns."

With rather characteristic understatement, he describes the feelings evoked by his experience at the Somme:

". . . trudging through the fields of mud around and through water-filled shell holes, dragging one or two reluctant animals behind us, with no cover from enemy shelling was frustrating . . ."

This time, the Artillery got it right. Casualties on the Canadian side dropped dramatically. After the 4th Division finally took Regina Trench on November 11, its General sent a letter to the Artillery commending them for "the very splendid way that your arm of the service co-operated with us"[6]. In fact, the artillery had co-operated so well that the objective, once taken, was useless:

"Regina Trench, the capture of which had cost so much blood, was no longer a position of strength. Repeated bombardments had reduced it to a mere depression in the chalk, in many places blown more than twenty feet wide, and for long stretches almost filled with debris and dead bodies." [7]

AMMUNITION COLUMN ON THE SOMME, OCTOBER 1916

> War Diary of the 3ʳᴰ Divisional Ammunition Column for October 28, 1916:
>
> No 1 Section whilst carrying ammunition to the 8ᵗʰ & 9ᵗʰ Brigades were heavily shelled by German Fire near the outskirts of Martinpuich. Casualties were: Killed 1 Sgt and 1 other rank; wounded Lieut. Hughson and 12 other ranks.

On November 18, the 4th Division were called upon to take a second German position known as Desire Trench. The weather was so appalling that the Artillery supporting the attack were practically firing blind into driving snow and sleet. Worthington describes the conditions:

> *"Soaked and coated with mud, men's clothing was so sodden as to add over fifty pounds to their carrying weight. . . . Long sopping greatcoats froze, knocked against ankles and tripped their wearers. Men who solved that problem by hacking them off at the knees were threatened with 'wilfully damaging His Majesty's property'."* [8]

But Driver Hesler was not cowed by the threat of military justice:

> "At this time we still had our Canadian great-coats which were splendid protection for the knees while the wearer was in the saddle but coming to within four inches of the ground they were impediments when walking through the mud as one stepped on the long skirt from step to step up and down muddy inclines. One night I became so worn out by such struggles that, regulations or no regulations, I took my knife and hacked away the surplus cloth but it did not tear well and ended up by being a comfortable length to the knees at the front while it barely covered my seat in the rear. This is what probably saved me from punishment for damaging the King's property as it did not look deliberate and I was able to satisfy enquiries by stating that it had been torn in disentangling myself from barbed wire."

In these miserable conditions, one of the few things to look forward to was a tot of rum. This courage in a bottle was rationed carefully so as to enhance the fighting spirit without impairing fighting ability:

> "We had earned the privilege of the rum ration when we first came to the Continent and it was now increased in frequency but there were still some teetotallers in the unit who did not imbibe this medicated firewater. However, they always drew their ration and either sold it immediately to comrades or hoarded it for a higher market. One late afternoon the word was passed that we would not be going up the line that night and the regular rum ration was ladled out. The hoarders now cashed in on an avid market amongst those who felt a need to celebrate this first reprieve from the mud fields of the forward area. By the time an emergency call came in about eight o'clock to rush ammunition to the guns, a half-dozen or so were in no state to walk, let alone mount or lead a horse or mule and next day's field trials brought varying degrees of punishment, one or two receiving the highest, F. P. No. l, of being tied to a wagon wheel twice a day and others were given pack drill."

Desire Trench was taken and became the last Canadian engagement on the Somme. Hesler writes:

> "Towards the end of November the 4th Division infantry and the three divisions of artillery withdrew from the area and headed north to the Vimy area where we were to be stationed for the next eighteen months, except for the Passchendaele excursion at the end of 1917."

By the end of November, the war returned to a situation of stalemate. Little had been accomplished. Over a 20-mile stretch of front, the German line had been pushed back an average of about four miles. Forgetting that the original objective had been territorial, Haig began touting the success of the operation in terms of the terrible attrition his forces had wrought upon the enemy. In a masterful piece of *ex post facto* rationalization, he reported that it was "beyond doubt that the enemy's losses in men and material have been very considerably higher than those of the Allies"[9]. The problem with that proud boast was that in actual fact, the enemy had suffered only half as many casualties as the Allies.

Of the 624,000 Allied dead and wounded on the Somme, 24,029 were Canadians. A British chronicler of the event writes:

> *"It is difficult to maintain a dispassionate attitude in recording such persistent aimlessness and unintelligence, for which the only penalty was the loss of other men's lives"*[10].

Thus the name of a modest French river quickly became part of the vocabulary of a great many families beyond the borders of France. To them it was a word, a sound, with dreadful connotations of suffering and loss.

HAIG MAKES A POINT WITH LLOYD GEORGE WHILE JOFFRE AND THE FRENCH MINISTER OF ARMAMENTS LOOK ON, DECEMBER 1916

It was not until after the war that people began to openly refer to the Somme as a fiasco. Most of the blame has to be handed to Haig. The rest lies with Sir William Robertson, who became Chief of the Imperial General Staff in December 1915 and the Cabinet's military adviser.

Robertson and Haig shared a common faith in the war of attrition, an abiding disdain for elected officials and a paralysing inability to get along with their French allies. Haig's biographer offers an insightful explanation for this last shortcoming:

> *"There are possibly no two races that experience greater difficulty in understanding one another than the English and the French. No few miles of salt water in the world have exercised so estranging an influence as the Straits of Dover. There is no natural antipathy between the races, nor did all the centuries of warfare ever breed a spirit of hatred; there is only a complete failure of mutual comprehension. They approach every problem from a different standpoint, and if they arrive at the same conclusion, they reach it by different roads. And perhaps the key to the enigma lies in the fact that the one quality they have in common is a deep-seated arrogance, which is too confident to breed boasting, but which at the bottom of the hearts of the inhabitants of both these countries assures them that they are superior to any other people on the earth. Hence they will make no effort to understand foreigners from whom they can have nothing to learn, and the Englishman can never be persuaded that there is not something slightly comic about a Frenchman, and the Frenchman remains convinced that the average Englishman is a fool."* [11]

As comical as these images may now seem, the fact remains that many thousands of lives were lost as a result of the pompous strutting and pettiness which went on for most of the war whenever the British and French high command attempted to communicate with each other on how to defeat their common enemy.

While the site and timing of the first assault at the Somme were not of Haig's choosing, the continuation of the attacks was entirely within his control. It is indicative of their own state of mind that his country's leaders allowed him to retain his command after such a disaster. Instead of re-appraising the whole situation and sacking Haig, they promoted him to the rank of Field Marshal and allowed him to repeat the disaster the following year at Passchendaele.

British Prime Minister David Lloyd George would have preferred to sack Haig, and his inability to do so is indicative of the strength of the military in British affairs at that time and the limited influence of the office of prime minister.

Lloyd George was a mercurial Welsh lawyer of extraordinary eloquence. He began his political career years before the war as a radical Liberal with a reputation as a pacifist and social reformer. He was utterly contemptuous of Haig. One method Lloyd George used in dealing with Haig was to repeatedly connive to subordinate him to the French High Command. The distrust and enmity between the leader of the British Government and the leader of the Imperial forces lasted throughout the war and could not have made for the most efficient prosecution of the British war effort.

The Canadian Corps was thus ultimately under the command of a man who espoused the doctrine of attrition and who enjoyed relative freedom from effective government control. Fortunately for the Canadian troops, their officers were somehow more successful in protecting their people from the slaughter than the others under Haig's command.

There may have been a number of reasons why the Canadian commanders were able to minimize the deadly consequences of Haig's stupidity. Some of these may have been rooted in a different social attitude, reflected in a genuine concern for the lives of subordinates. It may have been this concern which drove the Canadian officers, or at least enough of them, to *think* about what they had to do and how best to go about doing it. These same differences, however, did not do much to help the Australians and New Zealanders, who suffered more casualties than the Canadians with fewer men at the front. Perhaps the most important difference for the Canadians was the future Corps Commander, Arthur Currie, with his penchant for careful planning and his extraordinary ability to stand up to his superiors, including Haig himself. Currie was later described by one of his brigadier generals as having "an almost fanatical hatred of unnecessary casualties. Of all the men that I knew in nearly four years on the Western Front, I think Currie was the man who took the most care of the lives of his troops"[12].

By trial and costly error, the Canadians improved on techniques which they had begun using before they left the Somme. One such technique was the use of rolling artillery barrages which moved forward as the infantry advanced, depriving the Germans of the opportunity to resurface and man their guns as had occurred during the failed first attacks on Regina Trench. A McGill University chemistry professor turned Artillery Brigadier, Andrew McNaughton, perfected counter-artillery methods that pinpointed enemy guns by sound and flash recording. Tight coordination of the artillery in support of the infantry became the trademark of the Canadian forces. In the words of the Canadian military historian, Daniel Dancocks, "By 1917 the organization of the Canadian Corps Artillery and its ancillary services had reached an advanced stage that artilleries of other formations on the Western Front were unable to match to the end of the War."[13]

Another Canadian development was Brutinel's deployment of the machine gun in an offensive role similar to the artillery's. Through sheer determination, Canadian commanders saw to it that their units were supported by the maximum amount of material that could be either officially procured, commandeered through tough bargaining, or simply scrounged. By way of example, in May 1918 the average number of automatic weapons in a Canadian division was 1,557, compared to 244 in a British division[14].

The fact that the Canadians suffered fewer casualties than they might have cannot be ascribed to any good fortune in avoiding the worst of the conflict. The more they were successful, the more they were exposed. Lloyd George, with reference to the Battle of the Somme, remarked as follows:

> *"The Canadians played a part of such distinction that thenceforth they were marked as storm troops; for the remainder of the war they were brought along to head the assault in one great battle after another. Whenever the Germans found the Canadian Corps coming into the line they prepared for the worst."* [15]

The next such encounter was at Vimy Ridge.

CHAPTER FOUR

VIMY RIDGE AND LENS

The interval between the Somme and the assault on Vimy Ridge was a period of limited hostilities along the ten-mile sector of the Front held by the Canadian Corps at its peak strength of four front-line divisions[1].

> WAR DIARY OF THE 3RD DIVISIONAL AMMUNITION COLUMN FOR DECEMBER 11, 1916:
> Working Party of 90 men sent to Trench Mortars near Maroeuil during night.

"On Thursday, December 7th, I became one of a party of about a dozen men detailed to do some work for the Trench Mortar batteries. We spent the night at Maroeuil and next day took up quarters in the cellar of a non-existent house in Ste. Catherine where the road from Arras to Lens branches off. It was here that I 'celebrated' my 23rd birthday. Every day for a week we trudged through a communication trench to the front line running just beyond Écurie and Roclincourt, and worked on building a trench mortar emplacement ahead of the front line at a point where the German line was only yards away. On the day we finished our task by installing the mortar and bringing up ammunition which was a steel globe about the size of a basketball filled with explosives and with a steel shaft about twenty inches long, our hosts honoured us by firing a few ranging shots and then we withdrew a short distance to observe any reaction. Within a few minutes we could see "minnies"[2] flying through the air and with a few direct hits all of our work was undone and we returned to our unit at Frévin Capelle."

The Canadian Corps' second winter in Europe—and Driver Hesler's first—was the coldest on record for many years.

"On Monday January 22nd we moved a few miles from Frévin Capelle to Cambligneul where the animals had to stand in the open and the men found shelter in barn lofts. While we were here this section of France experienced the coldest winter in many years and as some bright officer had put through an order that all animals must be clipped, except for their legs, a number of them died from exposure and many were sent to the base to recuperate. Amongst the latter was Bang[3] of my team of Bing and Bang and I went down the social scale by being allotted a team of mules - but they were good mules of a copper color and I found that they were more intelligent than most horses."

One of the activities imposed on the soldiers to relieve the winter boredom was getting ready for inspection. Driver Hesler describes the consequences of trying to out-smart the Sergeant:

"Due to casualties at the Somme and other changes we now had several new officers and non-coms who had been transferred from other units. . . . The new sergeant in my sub-section was George Wilson, a graduate of Ontario Agricultural College, and being fellow Ontarioites we were on friendly terms but our friendship was strained by my abhorrence of harness cleaning. . . . The breaking point between George Wilson and me came when we were ordered to do a special job of polishing for an inspection by General Lipsett[4], the Divisional Commander. George was fretting all morning about the condition of my harness and was in a dither when the General stopped by my team and asked me where I hailed from. Knowing that he had commanded the 8th Battalion, Winnipeg Rifles, I replied that I came from Winnipeg, which was true in a certain sense. He then complimented me on the condition of my golden mules and the sheen of the harness which they bore. George and I remained good friends and after the war I saw him several times which is more than the occasions on which I saw others of the unit. However, he put the screws on me after the inspection mentioned by switching me to another team of mules and detailing us as part of a small group to join others from the Column to haul material on the light railway at Vimy Ridge."

Thus Driver Hesler's all-too-clever forsaking of his Ontario origins would lead him to become intimately familiar with a piece of French real estate temporarily expropriated by the German Empire, but later deeded in lesser extent by the Government of France to the people of Canada[5].

The Battle of Vimy Ridge has been described as "one of the most complete and decisive engagements of the war. The Germans were utterly defeated and driven from the field"[6]. It was also the first decisive victory for any British force in two and a half years. All this was in notable contrast with the costly deadlock clashes in which the Canadians had previously played a part.

The overall picture of events leading up to Vimy did not portend success. The British began 1917 by letting George V promote his friend Haig to the rank of Field Marshal, notwithstanding the disaster of the Somme. The French did the reverse by sacking Joffre, who had been successful in keeping the Germans out of Paris for two years, and replaced him with a new Commander-in-Chief, General Nivelle.

Nivelle had come into favour as a result of his spectacular counter-attacks at Verdun. He resolved to use the same tactics on a much grander scale intended to break through the German defences on a broad sector of the front along the River Aisne between Soissons and Reims. The plan was to abandon the strategy of attrition and replace it with massive shock tactics. It went awry as a result of delays which allowed the Germans enough time to complete their own innovative defensive strategy. This involved withdrawal to newly-constructed supporting fortifications known as the Hindenburg Line, and new defensive tactics based on mobility and entrapment instead of rigid confrontation along a set line of trenches vulnerable to artillery.

Niville went ahead with his planned offensive in April despite being warned by other French Generals (including the yet-to-be-infamous Pétain[7]), that it was no longer valid. The offensive failed as predicted, the French suffered casualties bad enough to provoke a general mutiny, Nivelle was sacked and Pétain took over.

Meanwhile, on April 9, the British under Field Marshal Haig had launched an offensive around Arras which was originally planned as a diversion for Nivelle's campaign. The role of the Canadian Corps in this effort was directed along the sector of the line in front of Vimy Ridge, as flanking support to a thrust by the British 3rd Army further south.

Vimy Ridge formed a natural barrier between the German and Allied positions north of the Hindenburg Line, and was one of the most important tactical features on the Western Front. In terms of observation and concealment, probably no other French real estate in German hands was as well suited to defence as Vimy Ridge. Thousands of French soldiers had died in two attempts to capture it in 1915.

In four days, the Canadians took and held the same heavily-defended positions which had held out against the far more costly offensives by the French.

The success of the Canadian Corps at Vimy was due mainly to planning and preparation of a degree not before seen on the Allied side. The fact that the whole Corps was engaged as a co-ordinated unit under General Byng helped accomplish this. The Corps' preparations for the attack on Vimy Ridge were the product of all the costly lessons learned up to that point. The commander of the 1st Division, Maj.-Gen. Arthur Currie, had earlier in the year visited the French positions at Verdun to study the methods used in Niville's successful counter-offensive. He and his colleagues under Byng then set out to improve on these methods. Currie helped develop procedures for effectively integrating the efforts of infantry and artillery. After the battle, members of the French General Staff revisited Vimy to see what they could learn from the Canadian action.

The attack was actually rehearsed over a full-scale replica of the site laid out to the rear of the Canadian lines. Nearly four miles of electrically-lit tunnels, called sub-ways, were dug 25 feet underground to the forward positions. Command positions and field hospitals were set up in underground caverns. Communications were assured by miles of telephone wire buried deep enough to resist enemy shelling. Daytime movement was camouflaged by dirt-coloured hemp banners strung across roadways on poles so that the roads looked empty from a distance on the ridge.

The "philosophy" of the Canadian plan was to spare no expense in resources of the material variety, as opposed to the human. The focus was on firepower rather than manpower. The artillery support was of a density and sophistication not previously seen. Augmented by British batteries, so much artillery was brought to bear on the Germans that there was one gun for every fifteen yards of frontage. The attack was preceded by three weeks of round-the-clock bombardment. More than a million rounds weighing 50,000 tons landed on the German positions. High explosive shells specially designed to destroy barbed wire were used for the first time. German guns out of sight behind the Ridge were targeted by counter-artillery directed by aerial observation and the sound and flash ranging systems developed by McGill's McNaughton.

Another method of gathering tactical information relied on the trench-raiding skills of the Canadians, which were put to use in the weeks preceding the attack, specifically to gather prisoners for interrogation. Had it not been for the need to gather intelligence, the reputation of the Canadians for taking few prisoners might have been worse. Unlike the Germans, the Canadians had no need of prisoners for labour on the home front. A live captured German was a logistical encumbrance. Most Canadians captured by Germans probably fared much better, even if the Germans considered them to be contemptible mercenaries who had no business being there. The German perception of the Canadians as mercenaries is an interesting one, particularly since any such thought seems to have escaped the minds of those who, like

Driver Hesler, voluntarily left a secure and safe job to fight in a foreign war for a dollar a day[8].

To sustain the artillery support for the Vimy operation, an unprecedented quantity of ammunition had to be run up to the guns in the weeks before. The Germans enjoyed an almost perfect panorama of the plain below them. Most of the supply activity had to be done at night to avoid being targeted. Closer in, noise was another problem to be overcome. Driver Hesler describes one precaution that had to be taken on the light railway that had been laid out to the gun positions:

> "Behind La Targette a line branched off to the field gun emplacements and was called the "Inner Circle" while the longer line was called the "Outer Circle". The Inner Circle was used sometimes in daylight but the other could only be used at night and when we got to the end of that line each driver had to stand over his mule and be ready to prevent him from hee-hawing to the Germans not far away."

MULE TEAM DRAWING AMMUNITION ON THE INNER CIRCLE NEAR VIMY, APRIL 1917

The aerial reconnaissance on which the artillery relied so heavily was vigorously harassed by German pilots. One of the more flamboyant and successful of these had painted his Albatross biplane red. Fortunately, lowly muleskinners like Driver Hesler were not considered fair game by the likes of the Red Baron:

> "One morning at daybreak I was alone on piquet watching over the mules when a German plane came into view over the nearby ruined tower at Mont St. Eloi flying from the east at a very low altitude. The pilot leaned out of his cockpit and gave me a wave of the arm and I recognized the face and plane of Richthoffen."

It was a dangerous worksite, even without the efforts of the enemy to make it so:

> "[Another] event occurred one morning when we were delivering ammunition to batteries on the Inner Circle. We were sitting on our mules in front of the guns which had been quiet when we arrived and should have been kept that way while their men were unloading our cars. Suddenly they began to fire and I was struck by the look of amazement on the face of one of the drivers on another team – the head of his mule had been cleanly sheared off by a defective shell. Something like a chicken, the mule remained standing for a minute or two. We were using a lot of American-made ammunition at this time and much of it was defective. Even we heard rumours of sabotage in the United States and many artillery men were nervous about using ammunition made there."

The attack on Vimy Ridge was launched at 5:30 on Easter Monday, April 9th. It was supported by a rolling barrage of nearly 1,000 artillery pieces and continuous fire from a concentration of machine guns unprecedented in military history.

Each event of the war produced its own terrible or awesome memory of the senses, and for most of the thousands of Canadians at Vimy, the most awesome was the sound of their own guns. Monumentally impressive to the distant observer, the thunderous noise of the barrage and the concussion in the air was truly horrendous to those living under it. Preceded by days of less concentrated bombardment, its effect on the psyche was practically hallucinatory. One description which survived the event was of "a solid ceiling of sound" that one could almost reach out and touch as if it "had the attribute of solidity"[9].

PACK HORSES TRANSPORTING AMMUNITION TO THE 20TH BATTERY, CANADIAN FIELD ARTILLERY, APRIL 1917

Over a four-mile front there were a myriad of engagements with German units who had survived the barrage, but this was no repeat of the Somme. The accuracy and timing of the artillery "lifts", combined with the hail of offensive machine gun fire, kept the Germans pinned down in their bunkers until they were over-run. In most places, not enough barbed wire had survived the high explosive shells to slow the attackers, and the German machine gunners lost the race to the parapet. When the attack outran its own artillery support, Canadian gunners turned captured guns on the German positions in the plain beyond the Ridge and bombarded them with their own gas shells.

On April 10, the German commander, the Crown Prince of Bavaria, wrote in his diary: "No one could have foreseen that the expected offensive would gain ground so quickly"[10]. The following day, he ordered a general withdrawal.

By April 14, the Canadians had consolidated their positions on the Ridge and in the Douai plain on the far side of it. Out of the 100,000 Canadians in the Canadian Corps, there were 10,600 casualties, 3,600 of them fatal.

The success of the Canadians in holding onto Vimy Ridge was almost as noteworthy as its capture. Nearly every other Allied gain that year would be lost before the end of the war. The threat of a German counter-attack remained constant, and preparations were taken to defend against it. Canadian artillery was positioned in the Douai plain to keep German guns out of range of the ridge:

> "The next day [April 15th] I had an interesting experience when about a dozen of us, mounted on single mules, trekked about 10 miles to the old gun positions, near La Targette, to pick up ammunition and move it forward. . . . My little group loaded up their packs and moved out over ground which was now drying out but still held uncollected corpses of men killed on April 9th. The plank road connecting the Arras-Béthune and Arras-Lens roads which we later used had not been built and we went across country through obliterated Neuville St. Vaast and then down the sloping road on the east side of the escarpment into Vimy village from which the Germans had retired on April 13 and was then occupied by our field gun batteries. Here we delivered the loads while the Germans started up a strafe of the gun positions. . . . Fritz must have seen my group going up the incline and by the time I got there he was shelling the road in a moving pattern which accompanied me most of the way but my mule was fast, and probably as frightened as I was, and we outran the range."

A gunner turned lawyer later wrote a book which contains a description of the same stretch of road at the same time:

> *"The long winding road down the east face of the ridge was in full view of the enemy and within easy range of their guns. Traffic had to be sent down in little groups so as not to present a solid continuous target that would mean that any*

*shell on the road was a dead hit. I well remember the sight
as I looked down from the top of the ridge waiting for our
turn to go. The whole thing was a clutter of smashed guns
and wagons, dead horses and dead men. . . No one who
saw that road during the fortnight following the capture of
the ridge will ever forget it."* [11]

ONE OF DRIVER HESLER'S MULES AT VIMY RIDGE, APRIL 1917

Driver Hesler's mule that outran the German shelling on the Vimy
Ridge road—or one of his other worthy steeds—was destined to become
more anchored in the memorabilia of war than most of the other 50,000
animals in the Arras sector of the Front. The disparaging reputation
for stubbornness and crankiness of mules generally is probably the
result of centuries of mistreatment due to the fact that they are not as
elegant an animal as the horse. Properly handled, the mule had more
strength and stamina than the horse, and was more intelligent and even-
tempered. There were, however, exceptions. Many years later, Hesler,
turned banker and bibliophile, was astounded to find what he believed
to be his mule's portrait, taken without his knowledge at Vimy Ridge
and credited to the Imperial War Museum in London, in a British
publication he had just come across in a Montreal bookstore:

"One of the mules assigned to me was a perverse animal
of strange appearance which delighted in rolling in

the mud and kicking anything in range. Somewhere, sometime, when I was not around a photographer was attracted by the unusual animal and took his picture which appeared in R. H. Mottram's "Journey to the Western Front", published in 1936 . . . This is the mule I drove on the light railway from Mont. St. Eloi to Vimy Ridge night and day for weeks in March and April 1917 . . . The man at the head is Bill Parkinson and the man at the tail is Brown . . . As can be seen this mule enjoyed rolling in the mud. He often tried it when I was on his back. . . . On Wednesday April 11th it was snowing rather heavily and I think it was on this day that my mule was photographed as it will be seen that there was snow on the ground at his feet."[12]

Like many common soldiers, Driver Hesler had more respect for certain mules than for certain officers, which is not to say that the officers were more deserving of respect:

"The Lieutenant in charge of the [ammunition] dump was dubbed "Puss-in-Boots". He always wore rubber boots and in his isolated hut must have been lonesome, for more than once he came out of his castle to halt a departing train and caress a mule with the explanation 'I love mules'."

After Vimy, Haig continued the Arras offensive and units of the Canadian Corps were involved in a series of hard-fought engagements at Arleux and Fresnoy eastward from Vimy Ridge. By the end of April, however, it became apparent to Haig that Nivelle's offensive on the Aisne would have to be abandoned, and that it would be pointless to pursue an advance that might outrun the French and become exposed on the right flank. Haig thus shifted strategy towards a consolidation of the line.

With the failure of the Niville offensive, French and British political and military leaders met at Paris and resolved that their strategy should return to the time-honoured objective of wearing down the enemy. Ypres would once again become the focus of Haig's planning. As a diversion from the shift of British strength towards the north, units of the Canadian Corps continued to raid German positions along the Souchez River near Vimy, in the direction of Lens.

> "On the 28th [of June] the 3rd and 4th Divisions began an offensive which was successful in pushing the line closer to the city of Lens which was straight ahead of us. Bouvigny Woods was at the western end of a spur running into the Souchez Valley, west of Lens, from which the Germans had been dislodged in 1915 by the costly French offensive of that time."

In July, Haig issued orders to Horne's First Army to take Lens itself.

In the meantime, on June 9, Byng was promoted to command the British Third Army. By this time, it was clear that the new Canadian Corps Commander would not be a British officer, but the decision was reached by the British with scarcely any consultation with the Canadian Government. Although he was not highest in seniority, the British chose Currie. Haig, in particular, was an admirer of Currie, despite the fact that Currie was far from complacent as a subordinate. Haig instilled a degree of awe and deference in his other subordinates which inhibited the giving of advice and allowed costly errors. Not so with Currie, who at six-feet-four and 250 pounds, towered above his superiors. When once asked by Haig for his opinion on a plan, Currie is reported to have replied: "Well, sir, I don't think it is worth a God damn"[13]. Currie's ability to stand up to Haig saved a lot of Canadian lives.

Currie came close to missing out on his promotion. From the moment he first saw action at Ypres II in 1915, he had been constantly exposed to the dangers of the battlefield. Three days before his appointment as Corps commander, his headquarters was destroyed by a direct hit and everyone in it was killed or wounded. Currie, unable to find a runner to carry a message over the open ground to his signals centre, had left a few seconds earlier to do it himself.

Currie's appointment as Corps commander coincided with a reorganization that saw Driver Hesler's section shunted from the 3rd Division to the 4th during the month of June. The first part of the summer was relatively quiet.

"As at Mont St. Eloi, we were again with open horse lines and bivouacs constructed by the men. With a team-mate, Dick Coller, I shared a small abode which we had built out of scrap material with chicken-wire cots making a comfortable shelter in the pleasant summer weather."

The only incident of note recorded during this moment of relative calm did not involve death at the hands of the Germans:

"I also recall the excitement of watching a British firing party march into the woods with a pair of convicted men and listening to the ensuing salvo of execution."

The prospect of death by firing squad was the ultimate dissuasion for anyone considering desertion. In the course of the war, twenty-three Canadians were marched out at dawn and shot by their compatriots in the manner recalled by Driver Hesler[14].

The most significant Canadian engagement in the interval between Vimy and Passchendaele was at a position dominating the town of Lens known as Hill 70. Lens was the centre of one of the main coal-mining regions of France. Its capture was intended to lure the Germans into expecting a massive attack on the major city of Lille, instead of Haig's planned northern offensive in the direction of Passchendaele. Currie was ordered to attack the outskirts of Lens, but responded that this would make no sense without first capturing the high ground which gave the Germans a clear line of defensive fire. In September 1915, the British had managed to take Hill 70, but had been driven off with terrible losses. Arguing that "if we were to fight at all we ought to fight for something worth having", Currie convinced Haig to change his orders and then talked him into diverting additional artillery from Ypres to support the Canadian attack.

On August 15, Hill 70 was assaulted by the 1st and 2nd Divisions in an operation reminiscent of Vimy Ridge. As at Vimy, the attack was preceded and supported by massive artillery. For the first time, artillery fire was directed by forward observers using wireless communication. Currie's preparations and tactics had been designed to first drive the Germans off the hill and then lure them back onto it and annihilate them. Over the next eight days, the Germans threw 69 battalions into Currie's trap and suffered 30,000 casualties.

The Germans retaliated with a new chemical weapon euphemistically known as "mustard gas". The mustard gas was particularly effective against the gunners and the men in the ammunition columns[15]. By that time, adequate protection against gas had been issued to the troops, but the new mustard gas contaminated protective clothing and produced unexpected problems. Driver Hesler appears to have come out of it not too much the worse for wear:

> "We made frequent trips up the line, increasing in activity in the preparation and support of the attack on Hill 70 near Lens which began on August 15 and ended with capture on the 25th. During this period one trip had varied consequences. As one of a party with about four ammunition wagons I made a trip after dark to our guns in Lieven, a suburb of Lens, and while there we were subjected to a bombardment of gas shells poured into the remains of buildings surrounding us. Shortly before this gas masks had been distributed for use on horses and mules with unusually humane instructions that the men were to don their own masks first in case of need. However, with that impediment over one's face it was quite a struggle to place masks properly on two mules and there was risk of displacement of the man's mask in doing so and the inhalation of gas."

Currie described Hill 70 as "altogether the hardest battle in which the Corps has participated"[16]. Casualties there and in the outskirts of Lens were almost as high as at Vimy, and many of them were from gas. On the other side of the balance sheet, the Canadians had gained another strong tactical position that would not again change hands, and the ratio of German casualties was four or five times higher than it had been at the Somme. A German military historian wrote that these German losses, combined with the threat of a continuation of the attack by Canadian forces, "upset the entire preconceived plan for relieving the troops in Flanders"[17]. Whether this made any impact on the horrific conditions endured at Passchendaele in the months to follow is unknown.

While all this was going on, Currie was having to undergo the pressures of a campaign waged at home and amongst Canadians in London to ruin him. Samuel Hughes, although kicked out of the cabinet, was still a powerful figure in the Canadian establishment, with even more powerful friends like the press baron, Max Aitken[18]. Currie owed his first brigade command to Hughes in 1914. However, it was Currie who had chaired the board of inquiry which led to the condemnation of Hughes' precious Ross rifle after Ypres II. Worse still, Currie was perceived as having tried to block the career advancement of Hughes' son, Garnet, not once, but twice. In 1915, when given the command of the 1st Division, Currie opposed Garnet Hughes' appointment as commander of the 1st Infantry Brigade. In June, 1917, Currie refused to let Garnet Hughes succeed him as commander of the 1st Division. Garnet Hughes and Currie were contemporaries and friends, and Currie's failure to put considerations of personal loyalty ahead of competence nearly became his undoing.

The biography written by Currie's friend and admirer, Col. H.M. Urquhart, suggests that the Hughes cabal saw to it that Currie's pre-war debts would come back to haunt him, threatening him with bankruptcy. Urquhart's theory was that Currie's creditors were prompted to suddenly demand payment of debts relating his West-Coast real-estate dealings. The truth of the matter is that Currie had temporarily pocketed $8,300 belonging to his old militia regiment in Victoria in order to avoid' bankruptcy when the real estate boom went bust just before the outbreak of war. It is tempting to speculate that this old skeleton was dragged out of the closet when Currie's enemies found the timing appropriate in 1917, but the likelihood is that the matter resurfaced of its own accord. In any event, faced with the prospect of Currie's disgrace and recall, two fellow officers bailed him out.

Quite independently of the Victoria matter, Hughes tried to unseat Currie by attacking him under the cloak of Parliamentary immunity with outrageously unfounded accusations of cowardice and incompetence. Aitken's British newspapers fed rumours of his imminent recall. The lack of proper press coverage in Canada of the Canadian efforts in the field undermined Currie's support at home. Borden and his government, fighting a bitter election over conscription and the war, and unwilling to take chances, avoided showing any outward support for Currie.

Towards the end of 1917, Currie made additional enemies within the ranks of idle Canadian officers in England by opposing the creation of a second corps and ordering the dispersal of the newly-formed 5th Division's manpower as badly-needed reinforcements for the other four. Again, Currie put military efficiency ahead of the personal aspirations of those eager for appointment. Currie's determination to resist diluting his divisions was a factor in the critical success of the Canadian Corps during the last one hundred days of the war.

ARTHUR CURRIE

Currie's ability to weather the storm created by his enemies at home and deal with the Germans at the same time was remarkable. He survived the storm mainly because of the tremendous respect in which he was held by both his subordinates in the field and the British high command.

Burdened only by the hostility of the Germans, Driver Hesler and his unit left their encampment at Bouvigny Woods five miles west of Lens on October 9 and headed north to familiar territory near Ypres.

CHAPTER FIVE

PASSCHENDAELE

In 1914, Passchendaele was a cross-roads village on a low ridge in Flanders of no particular note other than that it lay in the path of anyone wanting to travel from Ypres to the Belgian coastal towns of Ostend and Zeebrugge. Since the beginning of the deadlock in 1914, Sir Douglas Haig had wanted the British Army to do precisely that. It was from Ypres that Haig would have preferred to launch the 1916 offensive which, as we have seen in Chapter Three, was carried out instead at the Somme in response to the urgings of the French.

By mid-1917, there were a number of arguments at Haig's disposal to support his request that the British War Cabinet approve a strategic thrust from the Ypres Salient. Apart from the fact that it was the German invasion of Belgium that had triggered Britain's entry into the war in the first place, the North Sea coast at the eastern entrance to the English Channel was strategically important for a number of reasons. Indeed, the deadlock of 1914 had been preceded by a great "race to the sea", in which the opposing armies tried to outflank each other in establishing the northern limit of the front as far into the other's territory as possible.

By capturing the Belgian coast, Haig and his supporters hoped to put a crimp in German naval operations, and particularly the U-boat campaign which was assumed to be based there and which had escalated in the minds of some to the point of threatening the British Isles with starvation. In the first five months of 1917, the British merchant navy lost no fewer than 572 ships. It was only later revealed that the Belgian ports were of relatively minor importance to the U-boat effort. While the U-boat threat itself was perhaps exaggerated, it was a fact that by mid-1917, the German High Command had concluded that the submarine was their only chance of winning the war. Ironically, it was the escalation of the U-boat campaign in 1917 which brought the United States into the war in time for the additional manpower to tip the delicate balance between two exhausted forces in favour of the Allies.

Another technological impulse to the northern offensive was found in the civilian casualties from cross-Channel Zeppelin and Gotha bomber raids on London and Southern England. Finally, Haig surmised that a successful coastal campaign would bring the Netherlands into the war on the side of the Allies.

Whether other factors lay in the back of Haig's mind is a matter of conjecture. Constantly irritated by the dominant role accorded the French in the conduct of the war, and convinced that the German Army was near collapse, it may well be that he saw in his northern offensive the opportunity to achieve victory on his own terms and to become the ultimate hero of the Allied effort. Contemptuous of the French, Haig wrote: "There is no doubt to my mind but that the war must be won by the Forces of the British Empire"[1].

Lloyd George and other prominent British leaders like Churchill, were opposed to any repetition of the Somme *débâcle*. Lloyd George favoured instead the continuation of campaigns in other theatres of war like Turkey, Greece, Mesopotamia and Palestine. These "side-shows" had very little impact on the Germans, and their proponents found themselves arguing against Haig and Robertson with nothing more than a weak alternative to the doctrine of attrition.

The Cabinet held ultimate authority over major strategic decisions, but Haig had powerful support amongst its members, and the Prime Minister was constrained to rule by consensus. On matters of military strategy, even Lloyd George felt that he had to defer to Haig's advice. Lloyd George was conniving and inconsistent in his attempts to deal with Haig, but Haig was less than candid with the War Cabinet. Knowing that Lloyd George was opposed to a major offensive on the Western

Front unless the French did their full share, Haig deliberately concealed the fact that the French Army was in a state of virtual paralysis following the failure of the Niville offensive and the mutinies. Haig's Chief of Intelligence and confidant, Brigadier-General Charteris, consistently underestimated enemy strengths and over-estimated enemy casualties.

Canadian Prime Minister Borden later became privy to the deliberations leading up to the War Cabinet's reluctant decision:

> *"The British offensive of last year was obviously a mistake. Robertson and Haig urged it against the protests of the Cabinet. I have read the records of the Cabinet meeting of June 21st, 1917, at which Lloyd George examined with great ability the reasons pro and con and stated the opinion of the Cabinet that no such offensive should be undertaken. He said, however, that they must be guided by their military advisers and would defer to them if, after hearing all that was urged, they still thought the offensive should be undertaken."* [2]

After the war, Haig asserted that his ill-fated Passchendaele offensive had been in response to pleas from the French, but this was far from the truth. Pétain had told Haig's liaison officer that the plan was certain to fail. He personally urged Haig not to go ahead with it unless he was certain of success. Pétain's successor, Foch, described the plan to advance through the flood-plains of Flanders as "a duck's march" that was "futile, fantastic and dangerous". The French, Haig's opinion of them notwithstanding, were familiar with the geography and had come to know the business of dealing with the Germans, but the War Cabinet was not informed of their views of the situation. Finally, Haig used a *fait accompli* to clinch Cabinet approval by massing the British forces around Ypres and embarking on a successful preliminary assault on Messines Ridge.

Thus when history looks back on Passchendaele in light of Haig's machinations and rationalizations, that battle takes on even more sinister connotations than the disaster at the Somme. On this occasion, however, the recriminations began almost immediately. The fact that finally there was an outcry of revulsion at the futile slaughter was in part due to a general climate of exhaustion. Three years of war had produced over two million casualties amongst the British and Dominion forces on the Western Front alone. Scarcely a family in Britain or the English-speaking portion of the Empire was untouched. On the home front, privations were making life miserable.

There was at least one reasonable alternative to a northern offensive in 1917, and that was simply to mark time. Some people felt that if France needed to be saved, then the Americans could have a turn at doing it. Churchill demanded in the House of Commons that there be no further offensive until the Americans could make their presence felt. The United States had declared war on Germany in April, 1917, but it would not be until the following year that it would have an army on the Continent capable of making a difference. Many believed that it was time to simply hold firm until the Americans were ready. One has to wonder if Haig wanted to win the war himself before anyone else could share the credit.

While still waiting for Cabinet approval, Haig went ahead with the assault on Messines Ridge on June 7. With the Canadian diversionary attack in progress to the south at Lens[3], General Plumer's Second Army recaptured the ground which had been lost to the Germans at a cost of 1,373 Canadian casualties in April, 1916. The Battle of Messines Ridge began with the detonation of a million pounds of explosives in tunnels dug under the ridge. It was followed up with an assault modeled on the tactics employed by the Canadians at Vimy, but on a larger scale and equally successful. With the success of the Messines *fait accompli* in hand, Haig received reluctant approval to proceed with his overall plan, but on the condition that it not degenerate into another Somme type of static slugging match.

The capture of Messines Ridge left the ridge at Passchendaele as the next objective to be overcome in the march to the coast. Haig might have avoided the Passchendaele disaster altogether if he had followed up on the Messines victory in the manner indicated by more intelligent generalship. With the Germans temporarily in disarray, Plumer wanted to carry the offensive forward and take Passchendaele Ridge immediately. Plumer was one of the better British generals, but Haig rejected his advice at the urging of his favourite, General Gough. Gough felt that Passchendaele was part of the main action which had been promised to *his* Fifth Army, even if he would not be ready to exploit Plumer's success for another six weeks. In contrast with Plumer, who had been defending the Ypres Salient for two and a half years, Gough needed time to get to know the area.

This was all the Germans needed to regroup and get ready themselves. Convinced that the Lens diversion was only that, the Germans more than matched the British build-up with their new system of mobile deep defence based on special intervention divisions which were deployed to counter-attack any exposed advance. Instead of the old system of trenches, the Germans planted the muddy plain in front of Passchendaele with artillery-proof concrete pillboxes which bristled with machine guns.

The main assault was finally launched on July 31. A mammoth preliminary barrage hit the intentionally thinned-out German forward positions, but left the German rear guns intact with devastating consequences to the British infantry. Gough misconstrued Haig's inarticulately-stated objectives and the offensive veered off in the wrong direction. Within four weeks, the British suffered 68,000 casualties. Astonishingly, no one followed up on the condition which the Cabinet had imposed and which would have required an immediate cessation of the campaign. Instead, what had been touted as a grand coastal breakthrough became another gruesome succession of attacks with soberly proclaimed, *ex post facto* "limited objectives". By mid-October, Passchendaele Ridge was still in German hands.

Australian muleskinners at work near Passchendaele.
(Note the officer's contribution to the effort.)

Conditions on the ground had never been worse. It rained almost continuously. The drainage problems which the Canadians had first experienced when they relieved the French in front of Ypres in 1915 had been aggravated by two years of constant shelling. The wounded literally drowned before they could be helped. Many who were rescued died horrible deaths from gas gangrene spawned in wounds contaminated with bacterial filth. The dead could not be buried and the proliferation of corpses on the battlefield gave the survivors the impression that the slaughter was even worse than it was. The stench of gas residue mingled with that of rotting corpses over a vast, water-logged lunar landscape nearly devoid of recognizable features. The morale of officers and men alike sank to an all-time low. A visiting staff officer burst into hysterical tears at his first sight of the conditions. Sheer physical discomfort and fatigue made the prospect of death seem like a deliverance.

PACK MULES PASS BY A WRECKED ARTILLERY LIMBER NEAR YPRES,
31 JULY 1917

General Gough wrote that the "labour of bringing up supplies and ammunition, of moving or firing the guns, which had often sunk up to their axles, was a fearful strain on the officers and men . . . No battle in history was ever fought under such conditions as that of Passchendaele[4]".

Haig was apparently shielded from the realities of what Gough had seen, and never visited the front lines. With characteristic rationalization, Haig felt it was his *duty* not to visit the casualty clearing stations, because to do so might make him physically ill.

Just as the thunder of the guns was the most vivid memory of the senses from Vimy, at Passchendaele it was the stench. The Ypres Salient had been a theatre of continuous, concentrated battle since the first days of the war. With the aid of its low topography and previous agricultural vocation, it had become a veritable slough of filth. The natural odour of flooded pasture took on the even more pungent stink of thousands of decaying human bodies and parts of bodies, the excretions and other garbage of two million men living in water-logged holes in the ground for over three years, the rotting carcasses and waste from tens of thousands of horses and mules, and the totally new and equally sickening olfactory phenomena of chlorine gas residue and cordite. There was no escaping the smell. It was carried everywhere on the boots and in the clothing of the men. The men themselves stank and had no means of dealing with it. Infested with lice and plagued with hordes of scavenging rats, they endured.

On October 7, both Plumer and Gough advised Haig to close down the campaign, but Haig insisted that Passchendaele Ridge had to be taken. Failing to take the ridge would leave the British forces sprawled out over indefensible ground for the winter. Withdrawal to safer lines after so much bloodshed on wasted gains would provide Lloyd George with enough ammunition to finally get Cabinet support for sacking Haig. The Canadian military historian, Daniel G. Dancocks writes:

> *"However, Haig did have a trump card, and he proposed now to play it. This was Sir Arthur Currie's Canadian Army Corps. The victors of Vimy Ridge would be summoned to save Haig's battle, not to mention his reputation and, quite possibly, his career.*[5]*"*

After the successes at Vimy and Lens, Haig had formed a view of the Canadians to the effect that "though they have been opposed by the flower of the German Army (Guards, etc.) they feel they can beat the Germans every time"[6]. On October 9, a day on which the Australians suffered 7,000 casualties, Haig ordered the Canadian Corps to detach itself from the Vimy-Lens front and move north to Ypres. On the 13th, Currie was ordered to submit a plan for the capture of Passchendaele.

Five days later, the Canadians relieved the Australians, just as they had relieved the French two years previously. In the interval, the countryside had changed so much as to be unrecognizable. A Canadian staff officer made this comparison:

> *"The country itself was a wreck of its former self. Gone were the pleasant meadows, farm houses and copses. Nothing but a wilderness of mud and shell holes, dead bodies, and blasted trees."*[7]

The commander of the 4th Division, Major-General David Watson, wrote:

> *"No one of us, who had previous experience of the Ypres Salient fighting, could anticipate without horror and dread, the orders received for the great effort and still greater sacrifices of Passchendaele. The approaches to the front, and on beyond, were simply beyond description."* [8]

Nearly half the area was now bog. Artillery pieces to be taken over by the Canadians were mired in the mud. Rail lines and roadways had disappeared. Currie noted in his diary on the 17th: "Battlefield looks bad. No salvaging has been done and very few of the dead buried".

Driver Hesler, who had seen the area in its previous condition a year before, would have concurred:

> "On Monday, October 15th, we moved forward about 11 miles to open horse lines and makeshift billets near Vlamertinge. This area was now blanketed with horse lines and other camps, many more than in 1916, and the wet ground was churned up by countless hoofs of horses and mules. The Canadian infantry did not arrive in the forward area until October 22nd but we began immediately to prepare for the impending battle to capture Passchendaele Ridge.
>
> Our route to the guns lay through the city of Ypres where we picked up ammunition and packed it on the

backs of two mules or horses per man. Although the
city had been further levelled since we were last here and
the sogginess of the area behind it was disheartening
the view as one emerged from the eastern side of the
city, through Menin Gate, and crossed the moat-like
stream, was one of utmost destruction with nothing
but seas of mud and water being continually churned
by enemy shells, their explosions adding to the din of
our own guns, beginning with 15-inch pieces near the
city walls. . . . Outside the city a road branches off to the
right to pass by Hell-fire Corner, Hooge and Sanctuary
Wood on the way to the small town of Menin. The
left branch goes on to Zonnebeke and from its farther
extension a branch road runs to Passchendaele and
points northward. I passed along these latter roads
in 1938 when every field was green but the ground
was still uneven and piles of raked-up shells and other
war debris still remained, not as reminders, for anyone
having seen this area in 1917 needs no reminder of its
ghastly devastation."

GERMAN PRISONERS BEING MARCHED INTO YPRES
AS MULESKINNERS MOVE TO THE FRONT

The military police had the thankless task of controlling traffic
through Ypres in a way which would reap the least havoc from the
random killing meted out by German shelling:

> *"Directly it was getting dark and the ammunition columns would start up . . . When the whole column of them was on the cobbles on the straight road into Ypres then Jerry would open out with his long range guns and he'd get the range and drop shells along the road . . . All night long that went on until it started daylight. The road was absolutely a shambles with blood and gore and bits of horses . . . It was awful, really awful, and our orders were to shoot the drivers if they refused to stop so we could divide them up, so there was spaces in between."* [9]

One has to wonder how Currie felt about having to spearhead the tail-end of a campaign that was already a dismal failure, in quest of a useless objective. His first reaction when he was warned that the Corps might be sent north was outrage at what he thought was a horrible mistake. When his orders finally came, his only option, other than abandoning his men and his command to the British, was to do whatever he could to minimize the damage.

Currie's first move to that end was to flatly refuse to let the Canadian Corps be attached to the Fifth Army under Gough. Based on his experience at Regina Trench on the Somme, Currie thought Gough was incompetent. Haig might have treated Currie's refusal as an act of gross insubordination, but chose instead to acquiesce[10].

Then Currie prevailed on Plumer to once again try to dissuade Haig from continuing the futile offensive. Plumer appears to have thought that if anyone could convince Haig to back off, it would be Currie himself. Plumer arranged for Haig to visit Currie's headquarters where the Commander-in-Chief of the British forces and the former school teacher in charge of the Canadian Corps then talked in private. All Currie could extract from Haig were concessions on timing and artillery support. Haig advised Plumer that the resumption of the attack was not to take place until Currie was satisfied with the preparations.

The author of the official history of the Canadian Army in the war writes that: "There is ample evidence of Currie's skilled and forceful generalship and the efficiency of his well organized staff in the smoothness and despatch with which the preparations for the Canadian assault were carried into completion."[11] Currie set up his headquarters in a make-shift billet close to the front lines and reconnoitred the area in person in his usual fashion. On one occasion, a mud-splattered Currie returned to base and confronted a visiting Haig with his personal accounting of promised artillery which he had found missing. Currie commandeered sawmill equipment and what was left of local forests so that planked roads and gun platforms could be laid out over the mud like the corduroy roads of the Canadian backwoods. Guns were overhauled and new artillery positioned. Intelligence was gathered and German positions targeted for destruction. All this happened over a period of scarcely more than a week, under constant German shelling that produced more than 1,600 casualties amongst the men who toiled in the open, muddy approaches to the line. Driver Hesler was one of those whom the shrapnel spared.

> WAR DIARY OF THE 4TH DIVISIONAL AMMUNITION COLUMN FOR OCTOBER 20, 1917:
> 1 OR killed by shell fire near Ypres. 3 OR evacuated to Hospital, shell gas. Vicinity wagon lines bombed by hostile air craft, from 7-pm to 10-pm.

As at Vimy and Lens, the work of the artillery was to be the backbone of the attack in a massive expenditure of firepower, instead of manpower. Vast amounts of ammunition had to be run up to the 600 guns which were to lob more than two million shells at the German positions by the time the battle was over. Driver Hesler describes the conditions encountered by the divisional ammunition columns:

> "During this period we carried out various classes of duties but the worst was taking ammunition up the line. The main road was kept in fair repair up to a point where concentrated shelling broke it up. Beyond that, and off to the sides, the soft earth was honey-combed with water-filled shell holes and it was a neat balancing feat to find one's way at night through this maze, dragging two loaded mules behind, to a gun pit, particularly if it was 100 yards or more away from what was left of the roadway. We sometimes made two or three trips up the road from advanced dumps and it was gruelling and dangerous work which resulted in an

unusual number of casualties. Attempts were made to lay plank roads into the gun positions but the shelling was too intense to complete them, or if any progress was made, to maintain them."

Nowhere in Driver Hesler's *War Interlude* is there any reference to the suffering he witnessed, either in terms of what he saw or what he heard. Mingled with the deafening sounds of the guns and exploding shells were the sounds of men and animals dying in agony. One has to search elsewhere for descriptions of such horrible memories:

> *"From the darkness on all sides came the groans and wails of wounded men; faint, long, sobbing moans of agony, and despairing shrieks. It was too horribly obvious to me that dozens of men with serious wounds must have crawled for safety into shell holes, and now the water was rising above them and, powerless to move, they were slowly drowning."*[12]

> *"The mules were up to their bellies in mud. They couldn't get out. The drivers couldn't get them out. They couldn't get another step, and the mules brayed there in the darkness, you know, helpless. I have actually seen artillery drivers standing there crying, crying in their helplessness."*[13]

WOUNDED CANADIANS ON WAY TO AID POST, PASSCHENDAELE, NOVEMBER 1917

Of all the miseries endured at Passchendaele, the worst were reserved for the stretcher bearers. Often men who refused to take part in the killing on moral grounds, they were amongst the bravest and the strongest. They were exposed to the same continuous shell fire which randomly hit the ammunition columns and they wallowed in the same filthy mud, but they were in constant contact with the worst of what war could do to a human being. The horror of seeing and hearing those who could not be helped, the struggle to carry out in good time those who might just survive, and all this day after miserable day, made for an experience which had no real parallel. It is clear from the brief notations he made in his *War Interlude* that Driver Hesler had a great deal of admiration and respect for these men.

It was against this dismal background that one can picture the first Canadian attack which went in on October 26. The spot on the Ridge where the obliterated village of Passchendaele once stood was captured twelve days later in a step-by-step operation against the network of pillboxes and fortified positions which survived the artillery bombardment.

The arrival of the Canadians in itself had served as a warning to the Germans that a renewed attack was imminent, and they were ready to receive it despite the toll exacted by the preceding attempts. German resistance in terms of infantry, machine gun and artillery fire was vicious. Some Canadian attackers were strafed by German aircraft. Others were killed by their own guns.

The German determination to hold Passchendaele showed in the machine gunners who, rather than run, kept firing into the Canadian attackers until the last possible moment. The Canadians who survived gave the machine gunners no quarter and put them to the bayonet even as they raised their hands in surrender.

Exhaustion, casualties and mud rendered the initial efforts of the artillery less effective than usual, but by the time of the final assault, the Canadian guns were firing with speed and precision. An infantryman looking over his shoulder would see the pre-dawn sky ablaze with a ribbon of continuous muzzle flash, while to his front, the shells exploded in a creeping barrage that moved forward precisely fifty yards every four minutes.

General Watson gave the following account:

> "All below the Passchendaele Ridge, the German monster shells were flinging up masses of earth and water. Through all this the Canadians burst upon the enemy. They fought up to and around the crest village from which the village takes its name. They fought up to and captured blockhouses which were spitting streams of machine gun fire. They fought in the cellars, in and around the village of Mosselmarkt and on the Goudberg spur. The Germans could not withstand the fury of the onslaught. Shot down, bayoneted and prisoners, they yielded, and the attacking forces passed on." [14]

The capture of a portion of the ridge north of Passchendaele was completed on November 10. Four hundred and twenty Canadians were killed that day, most of them when the Canadian flank was exposed by two British supporting battalions who broke and ran under a German counter-attack. Currie was furious with the British. Finally Haig called a halt.

Looking north from Passchendaele Ridge, Canadian soldiers could see in the distance the green fields and undamaged villages that Haig had planned to roll through long before then, but which would remain in German hands until nearly the end of the war. The futility of it all would have seemed even greater to those same Canadians had they known that, five months later, the British would lose the ground they were standing on.

One concession that Currie had wrung from Haig was that, once their job was done, the Canadians would not be compelled to languish over the winter in the Flanders killing ground. On November 14 the Canadian Corps started returning to the Lens-Vimy front. Its month-long return to the Ypres Salient had cost 15,654 Canadian casualties, about as many as the Americans lost in battle during the entire Revolutionary War of 1775-1783.

Total British and Empire casualties during Ypres III were conservatively estimated at 260,000. Some suggest the figure is closer to 400,000. "Passchendaele", another terrible sound, this one with a Flemish bite to it, landed beside the "Somme" in the new English family lexicon.

Just as at the Somme, Haig had decided to go ahead with a plan that was predicated on an earlier start, the element of surprise and more favourable weather conditions. He ordered the attack in the absence of all three pre-conditions and persisted in it after all hope of success had disappeared. Instead of a breakthrough to the Belgian ports, Haig's forces had gained four miles of useless, desolate ground which later would be lost during the last great German offensive.

Currie and the Canadian Corps had been ordered into battle at Passchendaele without any consultation with the Canadian Government. After receiving Currie's account of the battle, Prime Minister Robert Borden met with Lloyd George and is quoted as saying: "Mr. Prime Minister, I want to tell you that if there is a repetition of the battle of Passchendaele, not a Canadian soldier will leave the shores of Canada as long as the Canadian people entrust the government of their country to my hands."[15]

Passchendaele was the most controversial battle of World War I. Churchill, not of the faint-of-heart, described the fiasco as "a forlorn expenditure of valour and life without equal in futility". Lloyd George referred to it as one of the "most gigantic, tenacious, grim, futile and bloody fights ever waged in the history of war"[16]. The historian, A.J.P. Taylor, called it "the blindest slaughter in a blind war"[17].

Notwithstanding Lloyd George's horror at the slaughter, firmer leadership on his part might have avoided the whole sorry saga. The fact remains that Lloyd George could have halted the campaign when it became obvious that the conditions that had been imposed by the War Cabinet had not been met.

Passchendaele was an event of such outrageous folly that it helped shape the minds of some who, in turn, helped shape a better world out of the chaos of the first half of the twentieth century. Lester Pearson was a fledgling fighter pilot recovering from a road accident in England when the reality of warfare was brutally driven home:

> *"I was soon well enough to be sent to a convalescent home
> and, later, was given leave until a medical board and the
> RFC decided what to do with me. This took time and I had
> six weeks of freedom from military life. It was a time I shall
> never forget. It was then that I became an adult. I began
> to think of things beyond the pleasures and excitements, the*

> *troubles and fears of the moment. I began to think, for the first time, about the war in its deeper significance and to realize its full horrors and gruesome stupidities, culminating in the bloody and pointless sacrifice of Passchendaele. My brother was there now. My other brother was flying a Camel. I would meet friends in London on leave from France and learn a few weeks later that they had gone for good."* 18

The compelling stupidity of Passchendaele was one of the lessons which later drove Pearson, as Canada's Minister for External Affairs, to take charge of a dangerous situation when Canada's old World War I allies, Britain and France, invaded Egypt in 1956. His initiative in calling for a cease-fire and setting up the first effective United Nations peacekeeping force earned him the Nobel Prize. His reaction to the Suez crisis was in stark contrast to the behaviour of the diplomats who might have prevented World War I. There were some similarities between the deadly posturing of 1914 and the hair-trigger stand-off of the Cold War. The costly lesson of Passchendaele was not lost on the man without whose timely intervention we might have had a third world war.

Passchendaele marked the end of three tough years of fighting for the Canadian Corps. Many thought that the war was only half over. As it turned out, there was only one more year to go, but it was to be the toughest.

CHAPTER SIX

THE FINAL YEAR OF BATTLE

While the Canadian battle front was cooling down for the winter, things had been heating up at home. The country's first conscription crisis began with the passage on August 29, 1917 of the Military Service Act. The Borden government found conscription necessary to sustain a war effort which was no longer devoted to just serving the "Mother Country". Waging war against the enemy of the imperial power was becoming a means towards colonial emancipation. The greater the success of Currie's Canadian Corps on the battlefield, the stronger became Borden's assertions for eventual full nationhood.

The problem with sustaining this new posture was that enlistments were falling short of casualties. A very sizeable chunk of the young adult male population of English-speaking Canada had already signed up. In 1914, the population of Canada was about 8 million. There would have been about 1.5 million males of military age fit to serve. One in three had already done so, and more than a third of them had been killed, wounded or taken prisoner. The enthusiasm of the remaining pool of eligible volunteers was chilled by the length of the casualty lists on the post office walls and in the newspapers.

Conscription was the central issue in the election which ran from December 1 to 17, 1917. The government loaded the dice in its favour by passing the War-Times Election Act which disenfranchised Canadian citizens of enemy birth or extraction if they were naturalized after 1902, and gave the vote (for the duration of hostilities) to the female relatives of Canadian servicemen, living or dead, including even those in the British forces. Great care was taken to ensure that the vote of every soldier at the front or in England was gathered in, for the right party, and then some. Driver Hesler voted while on leave in London in early December and could have done so again on the train returning to the front a week later:

> "A general election was set for December 17th and polling of overseas soldiers commenced on December 1st. This involved a peculiar method under which we were not allowed to vote for a candidate by name but only by party affiliation. While in London I voted for a Union candidate in Winnipeg Centre who turned out to be Major G. W. Andrews and he received the highest majority in the country.
>
> . . . Our train left Boulogne at 5 A. M. and took us directly to Béthune where we arrived at 10.30 A. M. This was the next-to-last day for polling the soldier vote and during the journey I was surprised to see an officer making his way along the running board outside the car which was not of the newer inner-corridor type. He entered our compartment and solicited votes and when I told him that I had already voted he shrugged that off but I refused to submit – honest old soldier."

NURSING SISTERS AT A CANADIAN FIELD HOSPITAL VOTING IN THE FEDERAL ELECTION OF 1917

The outcome of the election and conscription led to bloody riots in Quebec and a lasting climate of bitterness over the war. Notwithstanding the formidable contribution of units like the Vandoos, most French Canadians were not easily convinced that they should risk their lives to save a "Mother Country" which was not theirs. They were equally unenthusiastic about saving France. Their attitude was no different from that of the millions of Americans who saw no justification for plunging into Europe's mess until German U-boats started sinking their ships.

In the end, about 100,000 reinforcements were raised through conscription, but only about 24,000 ever saw continental Europe—about one for every conscript that defaulted and was either jailed or on the run for the remainder of the war.

Another event brought the war into tragic focus for Canadians at home. On December 6, 1917, a French munitions ship exploded in Halifax harbour, destroying a good part of the city and killing over 1,600 people.

When Driver Hesler returned to the front from his London leave, his commanding officer was getting ready for a new type of war:

> "I found that our Colonel, notwithstanding the failure of the British to break through at Cambrai, was apparently of a mind that 1918 would be a year of open warfare. Events proved him to be right in his judgement but if it was formed as loosely as his methods of preparation it could have been nothing but a lucky guess. On this day [December 17] I found that we were ordered to don gas masks just before putting the feed bags on the animals so that they would become accustomed to being handled by necessarily grotesque humans during gas conditions. To add to the simulated war scene a firing party of four men with rifles was stationed in the stable enclosure and ordered to discharge a few rounds while the rest of us struggled to put nose bags on the heads of mules, some of which showed by their complacent expressions that they thought that we were simple fools while others, not forgetting that they were veterans of the hell-fire of Passchendaele showed their disdain for mere rifles and gas masks by giving a merry hee-haw."

The mules were not the only hardened veterans. Nearly two years in a variety of living conditions had changed Driver Hesler's perception of comfort:

> "On December 21st we moved about three miles nearer to the front and took over good brick-floored and covered stables at Ablain St. Nazaire. . . . While our animals were well-provided with stables there was little provision for the men and everyone set to immediately to organize into groups which would forage for materials and build the numerous shacks in which we would live for the next three months. I joined five others, who between us, had prior rights to a large tarpaulin and before dark we had a comfortable wooden-walled home complete with wire netting beds and an oil drum stove. In this setting we prepared to celebrate our second Christmas at the front."

CHRISTMAS CARD SENT BY DRIVER HESLER TO HIS PARENTS BACK HOME, DECEMBER 1917

One of the few mementos Driver Hesler kept of the war is a sample of the Christmas card which the men of the 4th Canadian Division could send home from these most unfestive surroundings. The front of the card shows a Canadian infantryman in a fur jacket, rifle and bayonet at his side, peering with a grin under falling snow, through a shell-hole blasted in the rubble of a brick wall. On the wall, there is a plaque which reads "Ypres . . . Somme . . . Vimy Ridge . . . Lens". On the inside of the card, there was printed: "With Every Good Wish For Christmas And The Coming Year . . . 1917 . . . 1918."

During the winter of 1917-18, Montreal and Toronto were the only cities in Canada with a population larger than the concentration of Canadian soldiers in the area near Vimy Ridge. Most of the residents of this new agglomeration had little freedom of movement, but there were exceptions:

> "We had received reinforcements after our losses at Passchendaele and my team had been allotted to another driver while I was on leave in December so for most of the remainder of the war I was somewhat of a driver emeritus and went on many excursions, usually on a horse, officially and unofficially, alone or in charge of a group of men, animals and wagons, from the forward area to well behind the lines, wearing no insignia of rank, but I was never challenged and never carried a pass except when on leave. . . . Frequently on the pretext of exercising a horse I would ride over the old battlefield back to Château de la Haye or Carency or on foot explore the Lorette Ridge, Ablain St. Nazaire or Souchez."

The new year would indeed bring a new kind of open war like Driver Hesler's colonel predicted, but not much would be seen of it until late in March.

> "It was a very quiet winter with very little activity on the front of the Canadian Corps from Hill 70 to opposite Vimy village, movements being limited to several interchanges of divisions. There were some working parties but with spring breaking early some of our farmer boys were put to ploughing the hillside behind our camp in preparation for the planting of potatoes and other army food crops. Who would harvest them? We played with the fantastic thought that we might

remain here for the summer, almost reconciled to the belief that the war would go on forever, in ignorance of the great German thrust coming on both flanks in March and April to threaten the hold on the ridge ahead of us."

The ordinary soldier may indeed have been blissfully ignorant of what was afoot, but it did not come as a complete surprise to the higher echelons. From the beginning of the year, Currie had implemented a strategy of probing the German positions in front of the Canadian lines, harvesting prisoners for interrogation:

"Prisoners captured in our raids stated that all the Divisions had been brought up to strength and were undergoing hard training in the tactic of semi-open warfare. They stated, or left it to be understood, that the forthcoming German attacks were based on very deep initial penetration and the rapid exploitation of success." [1]

WAR DIARY OF THE 4ᵀᴴ DIVISIONAL AMMUNITION COLUMN FOR JANUARY 26, 1918:
Returns of men with knowledge of German called for.

What in fact occurred was a last desperate gamble. By the start of 1918, the Germans under Ludendorf had come to the conclusion that continuing to maintain a defensive position at the casualty rates inflicted by Allied offensives like Passchendaele would lead to eventual exhaustion and defeat. Ludendorf chose therefore to launch his own massive offensive, and to do so before the American presence could make up for Bolshevik Russia's withdrawal from hostilities following the "October Revolution".

Rather than one concentrated thrust on a narrow front like Haig would have attempted, the Germans spread their offensive out over almost the whole length of the line from Passchendaele in the North to Verdun in the South. With Russia out of the conflict, the Germans at last enjoyed the advantage of fighting on one front instead of two.

One of the few segments of the line they chose not to attack in strength was the 16-mile stretch held by the Canadian Corps near Vimy. Currie's insistence on maintaining a single corps and reinforcing instead of diluting its divisions as the French and British had done, left the four Canadian divisions the strongest ones in the line. Evidently the Germans had learned from experience that the Canadian sector would not be the point of least resistance. Borden described their state of readiness as follows:

> *"You would be greatly inspired by the wonderful prestige of the Canadian Army Corps. It is admitted that it is the most effective and reliable fighting unit of its size in the British forces. In reality, it is almost as strong numerically, and certainly as effective for either offence or defence as any of the British armies, although each army is supposed to comprise two army corps. Our battalions are at full strength, 1100 or more. Each of our divisions contains twelve battalions and we have stronger forces of machine gunners than the British."* [2]

Currie used a bit of bluff to reinforce the German perception of the odds against them:

> *"The Front held by the three Divisions then in the Canadian Corps had a length of approximately 29,000 yards; and of necessity the line was held very thinly and without much depth.*
>
> *To deceive the enemy regarding our dispositions and intentions, we adopted a very aggressive attitude. The Artillery constantly harassed the enemy's forward and rear areas and our Infantry penetrated his line at many points with strong fighting patrols and bold raiding parties. Gas was also projected on numerous occasions."* [3]

Ironically, by leaving the Canadian Corps relatively untouched in their spring offensive, the Germans sealed their fate. In the final one hundred days of the war, it was the highly efficient Canadian divisions under Currie which spearheaded the Allied offensive and finally broke the will of the German Army and its leaders to continue the fight.

Things would have gone differently if Haig had got his way. Looking as usual only at the constraints of the moment, Haig wanted to split up the Corps and place its divisions in support of the British forces in their retreat from the German spring offensive. Currie, with backing from Borden and the British War Secretary, resolutely resisted these attempts. A cable from Borden warned the War Secretary that "any proposal to break up the Canadian Army Corps would be strongly resented in Canada and would have the most unfortunate effect upon public opinion"[4].

The past successes of the Corps fighting as one unit gave the British government reasons to support Borden and Currie "on purely military grounds—and apart entirely from considerations of national sentiment". Haig noted in his diary that "I could not help feeling that some people in Canada regard themselves rather as 'allies' than fellow citizens in the Empire".

This whole incident may be interesting in tracking the development of a Canadian national identity, but it also shows that something else was beginning to gain respect: the opinion of the public.

In any event, through the reputation they had gained in earlier sacrifices and Currie's determination, the Canadians avoided dispersal and were mostly spared the consequences of the first great strategic advance since the deadlock began at the end of 1914.

For the British and French, it was a near disaster. The Germans used new tactics of infiltration, which resembled their elastic defence techniques, but in reverse. The British, on the other hand, had attempted to develop their own variety of elastic defence, but the result merely scattered static defence points without adequate mobile support.

Robert Borden, in a letter he sent home from London the following June, gives some insight on the state of British preparedness for the attack:

> *"If the British Army Corps had made the same preparation to meet the German offensive as did General Currie and the officers and men of the Canadian Forces, the German offensive could not possibly have succeeded as it did. Their*

losses would have been so appalling that they would have been obliged to stop.

. . .

The British higher command believed that the Germans would not undertake an offensive. Three days before it began the Chief Intelligence Officer gave the Canadian Corps a tip that they need not expect an offensive from the Germans. Currie told me that the reports of the Chief Intelligence Officer at British Headquarters were so useless and misleading that when he recognized the signature he always tore them up and threw them into the waste-paper basket without reading them." [5]

Starting on March 21, the Germans overran all the earlier gains of the French and British in the Somme area in less than two weeks, pushing the line back as much as 40 miles and threatening Amiens. Small detachments of Canadian cavalry and Brutinel's Motor Machine Gun Brigade were involved briefly, and the latter were instrumental in preventing a rout of the British in front of Amiens on March 26.

In the North, the British lost Messines Ridge and Passchendaele Ridge by April 17th. In less than a month, the British suffered 240,000 casualties.

Next, on May 27, the Germans turned again on the French, and in less than ten days, opened another vast bulge in the line right to the Marne, less than 40 miles from Paris.

Finally, on July 15, the Germans attempted a final thrust at the French capital in a repeat of the events of the second month of the war. But, as Stuart Robson puts it, "Ludendorf was winning his way to defeat"[6]. The offensive had by now consumed much of what was left of the best German troops. The French, with the support of four American divisions, counter-attacked. By August 7 the Germans were forced to withdraw to their starting positions, just as they had done in 1914. At a cost of one million casualties, Ludendorf's gamble had failed and German self-confidence was irrevocably shattered.

> WAR DIARY OF THE 4ᵀᴴ DIVISIONAL AMMUNITION COLUMN FOR
> MARCH 26, 1918:
> At 2.am. orders received to 'stand to' & be prepared to move at 1.0
> hours' notice.

All this great turmoil unfolded to the north and the south of the
Canadian positions, leaving them relatively untouched. However, until
the actual storm broke, the prospect of a German offensive hung over
the Canadian Corps like a cloud. Convinced that retreat was imminent,
the Colonel of Driver Hesler's unit began preparing for the worst. With
his flair for the dry comedy of war, Hesler describes his role in conveying
the order to stand firm:

> "[The Colonel] told us that he had learned that the
> enemy would soon be upon us and he wished to establish
> emergency measures of communication in the event of
> a break-through. He asked whether any of us knew
> where our Divisional Artillery H.Q. was located. It had
> been my firm policy since enlistment never to volunteer
> for anything but here in this "dramatic" moment I
> was caught within the silence of the others and broke
> down to declare that they were at Noeux-les-Mines .
> . . Accepting this, the Colonel majestically directed
> me "You will report with this message (handing me a
> sealed envelope) to the Staff Captain and be attached
> to H.Q. as liaison between it and me. You and your
> horse-holder will proceed there as quickly as possible
> without galloping your horses on the hard pavements".
> We set off immediately so I never knew what orders the
> others received. Down to Souchez and then parallel to
> the front line we followed the deserted Arras-Béthune
> road. An occasional flare over on the right was the only
> sign that men were mad at each other except for the
> devastation dimly discernible in the night. To break the
> monotony we broke the rules by galloping our horses
> for brief spells . . . The seven or eight miles were soon
> accomplished in Noeux-les-Mines, a town relatively free

from destruction but now in complete darkness, leaving me uncertain as to where H.Q. were located. Finding a sentry we obtained directions and warnings that Head Quarters did not like to be disturbed at night. The house to which we were directed was in total darkness but a spot of light in the garden turned out to be a Signals station with a man on duty. He directed me to the proper door of the chalet with further warnings about wakening people at 4 A. M. Undaunted, I rapped loudly on the massive front door and soon was rewarded by a candle-light appearing on the stairway, held in the hands of a woman, and when she came to the door the light she carried revealed such a charming lady as to give another meaning to the warning not to disturb the military at night. Without hesitation she accepted my request that I be taken to the Staff Captain and led the way up the stairs to a junior officer who was aroused with some difficulty. Apparently impressed by my insistence that I must see the Staff Captain personally, but not without a further warning, we went together and roused the sleeping warrior. He read the message which I had presented and burst into such profanity that even I, a muleskinner, felt admiration: "Your . . . Colonel says we are going to retreat this morning. Who in hell told him what the Germans are going to do? You get the hell out of here and go back and tell your Colonel from me that he's a goddamned fool". Well, anyway the lady went to the door with me. We decided to return to our lines by coming round the mountain in a different direction so that we could have coffee and eggs in Hersin-Coupigny—somehow the emergency did not seem so serious now. This delayed us in getting to our lines until about eight o'clock and here we found the entire Column hitched in and packed up ready to march, apparently waiting for me to come back with the directions for our flight. I delivered my message, edited, to the Colonel who, quite plainly disappointed that we were not going to retreat, gruffly ordered that the parade be dismissed."

The fear of being over-run, as the British had been, persisted. The Canadians kept on their toes:

"The Canadian Corps was stretched out from below Arras to near Lens and there was great anxiety over its ability to withstand a concerted push across Vimy Ridge. Reinforcements were being gathered from all sources and additional defences were being hastily prepared against possible renewed assaults against the ridge. As part of these activities I was sent out at the head of a gang of men to clear a cross-country road and bury a telephone wire from the Nine Elms (which had disappeared from the scene east of the Arras-Lens road) to the Arras-Béthune road as an additional exit for our guns in case the line broke. Digging into the old trench systems for material to fill shell holes we uncovered what was left of British, French and German soldiers who had never had any burial other than that provided by hasty construction of trenches and who had lost all means of identification."

General Currie's report on the operations of the Canadian forces during this period shows that Driver Hesler's labours were part of a much larger plan:

"A great deal of care was given to the distribution of the artillery in relation to the policy of defence. Three systems of Battery positions were built so as to distribute the guns in depth and sited so as to cover the ground on the north-east, east, and south, in case the flanks of the Corps should be turned.

Successive lines of retirement were also prepared, battery positions were selected, organised, and marked, cross-country tracks were opened up, and observation posts, echeloned in depth, were located and wired in." [7]

One of the oddities of the first world war was the kite balloon. Employed by both sides in the hundreds all along the front, they did what unmanned drones and satellite cameras do today. Those with enough nerve to venture aloft in these easy targets got a perk denied the crews of most winged aircraft at the time—the parachute.

"The line from opposite Arras to opposite Lens had been drawn back only slightly in the push which had started on March 21st but there was great intensiveness during all of these days . . . The days were bright and clear and our observation balloons were up every day. There was a string of six one day stretching out between Arras and Lens overlooking the Douai plains when a fast single-seater German plane swooped down from nowhere and starting at the northern end of the line he wove under and over alternate balloons firing a hail of bullets at each one. At the southern end he turned and went back over his work to finish off any bags that were still aloft. It was all done so quickly that every bag was down before it could be pulled down or defensive measures taken other than bailing out by the observers and the German was away to his own lines untouched. It was an admirable piece of work but the burning balloons would have delighted only a pyromaniac on our side."

WAR DIARY OF THE 4ᵀᴴ DIVISIONAL AMMUNITION COLUMN FOR APRIL 1, 1918:
During the day, the observation balloons near the camp were shelled by the enemy, and one horse on D.A.C. strength wounded by falling splinters. In the afternoon an enemy airman attacked the balloons mentioned, and brought down four.

Despite the intense activity which beset the other Allied armies to the north and south, the threat of being over-run was short-lived for the Canadians:

"The threat of disaster waned and although there was a fresh attack on the Somme to the south of us and renewed assaults to the north, the real threat of a break-through had come to a standstill by the end of April. The Germans had, however, practically destroyed towns which we had known in earlier days, such as Béthune and Bailleul . . ."

During this same period, Driver Hesler's unit withstood another kind of attack that would wreak havoc on millions over the next two years: the so-called Spanish flu[8]. Exposure to the pandemic in its less potent early phase, and the resulting immunity, may have been a blessing in disguise.

WAR DIARY OF THE 4TH DIVISIONAL AMMUNITION COLUMN FOR APRIL 1918:
An epidemic of mild influenza spread through the Camp, beginning approximately April 15th. By the end of the month disease had practically disappeared.

The next three months were the calm before another storm. Canadian commanders used this period to train their units in deadly earnest for the turning of the tide. Army officers have always been fond of the safe power trip of a military exercise, but the common soldier—particularly the kind who has seen real battle—tends to find such mock battles rather silly:

"For nearly three months we were to be out of gunshot (Big Bertha was trained on Paris) enjoying glorious summer weather and turning our minds to the possibility of a great Allied offensive with our Colonel again in his glory directing training for open warfare. . . . One fine afternoon the Colonel staged a great sham battle along the road that runs from Acq to Haut Avenes and the farm land lying on either side. We did not parade all of our wagons and animals but the drivers thus released, including myself, were armed with rifles and rode on the limbers. Thus arrayed and seated on the hot steel of wagons we were startled to see the Colonel mounted on his galloping horse rushing along our line firing his revolver into the air and shouting that the enemy was upon us. We riflemen were ordered to spread out through the fields to protect our line of wagons. After a period of aiming and snapping empty rifles some of us fell asleep in the convenient shooks of fodder that was being cut by the farmers while others chose to regard the farmers as the enemy and set them running at the ends of rifles."

Driver Hesler's recollection of events like these, forty-five years later, suggests that it is the lighter scenes of war that the mind chooses to retain, while the darker moments are allowed to slip from one's memory. Another anecdote from this period deserves mention. To fully appreciate its meaning, the reader should remember that Driver Hesler had been living for two years in a world where nothing could be expected to remain the same for long. Someone who was a comrade one day might be dead the next. A town or village visited on horseback for a meal or a beer in 1916 was a pile of debris in 1918. Even the bare landscape changed. Least likely to survive for long in this maelstrom were the tens of thousands of horses and mules that toiled through it for months on end. However, in any environment, there are always survivors:

"While we were here the Captain fell into a horse-trading mood and scouting around, found an Imperial unit that had some greys—our color scheme in horses was as always, grey. . . . One of the horses seemed familiar but I doubted that it could be old Bang that I had brought over from England two years earlier. Putting him to the sure test of mounting and touching his rump, identification was completed by the same old kicking and plunging that I had known until he faded in the severe winter of 1917 and was sent to base. I thought then that he would end up in a glue factory but here he was, still thin and somewhat greyer. A small world, even among horses."

The humour reflected in these reminiscences should not distract from the reality that the Canadians faced in the summer of 1918. The rumours of a great Allied offensive did not leave much to the imagination as to which forces would spearhead the attack. Soldiers have a sense for when it is their turn in the line. The Canadians knew they were ready, and much more ready than anyone else. On June 15th, Borden wrote that:

> *"The Canadian Army Corps is admittedly the most formidable striking force in the allied armies. Probably it is the best organized and most effective unit of its size in the world today. It has come on wonderfully since last year and this is due not only to the courage, resourcefulness and intelligence of the men, but to the splendid and unremitting work of the officers, and to Currie's great ability. I believe he is the ablest Corps Commander in the British Forces; more than that I believe he is at least as capable as any Army Commander among them."* [9]

Towards the end of July, at the same time as Ludendorf was contemplating the withdrawal of his forces from the Marne, the Canadian Corps moved out of the Vimy-Lens sector and began moving secretly by night forty miles southwards to Amiens. It was from there that the Canadians would launch the first in a series of attacks that became known as "Canada's Hundred Days".

In the last four months of the war, more than 42,000 Canadians became casualties, but the damage inflicted on the enemy was staggering. From August 8 to October 11, Currie's four divisions successively engaged and defeated elements of forty-seven German divisions, or nearly a quarter of the German forces on the Western Front. By November 11, the Canadians had liberated 228 cities, towns and villages and occupied more than 500 square miles of enemy territory, including the cities of Cambrai, Denain, Valenciennes and Mons[10]. The British, Australians, French and Americans achieved gains as well, but none so spectacular. The Canadian breakthrough shortened the war, just as earlier Canadian successes may have prevented it from ending unfavourably. In large part, this success was due to Currie's organizational and leadership skills. Another factor was that the Canadian effort was part of the first properly coordinated Allied grand offensive. Amiens was to be the first phase.

The realities of the dangerous situation in which the Allies found themselves in March had led to the appointment of Foch as the Supreme

Commander of the Allied forces. The Amiens offensive was planned by Foch as a joint British and French operation under Haig, supported by massive artillery support, over 600 tanks and over 2,000 aircraft. The Canadian Corps was positioned at the centre of the German line immediately in front of Amiens, with the French on the right and Australians and British to the left. The main blow was to be struck by the Canadians, supported by British tanks. Launched at 4:20 on the morning of August 8, the attack was a complete success. The stealth with which the Canadians had moved into position and the absence of a preliminary artillery barrage left the Germans completely surprised. The guns firing over the heads of the attackers neutralized the enemy's artillery and pinned down the defenders until they were overrun. The success and speed of the advance created a new challenge for the artillery: moving forward quickly to keep pace with the attack.

Just prior to the move to Amiens, Driver Hesler had the good fortune to become the assistant to his unit's acting quartermaster-sergeant, and from then until the end of the war, he was no longer called upon to run ammunition to the front lines. From this more leisurely vantage point, he recalled his experience at Amiens:

> "Setting out again at nightfall on Monday, August 4th, we crossed the River Somme and encircled Amiens so that by daybreak we were securely hidden in the woods in front of Boves, about 6 miles south-east of Amiens. The woods were full of troops and all were cautioned to keep under cover. Fires were not permitted and with a penetrating rain falling on the night of the 5th through the 6th it was very uncomfortable. I had my usual jobs to attend to and kept busy. During the night of the 7th our ammunition wagons started out to take up their positions for the expected break-through next morning. With the remaining wagons I left the woods about 4.30 in the morning of the 8th and halting on the high ground at the edge of the woods we saw the great outburst of firing that opened up this great battle. Remaining here until word came back for us to move up we occupied grand-stand seats for a great spectacle. Moving off, we progressed slowly, stopping for some

time to lend a hand at a forward ammunition dump and eventually arrived at the point where our forward wagons had made camp in what had been no-mans land twelve hours earlier. Our line had advanced 8 miles during the day and progress was continuing. Everyone had taken on new life and the appearance of cavalry changed the scene of previous dull warfare."

Ludendorf later wrote that "August 8th was the black day of the German Army in the history of this war"[11]. It was an even darker day for Ludendorf. The defeat at Amiens was the beginning of a series of events which would soon bring the monolithic "Genius of World War I" to a state of complete psychological collapse. The Germans had been thrown back eight miles in the centre of the attack by the Canadians. The Australians had accomplished nearly as much, with the British and French making more modest gains. The cost in Canadian casualties was relatively light: about a third of the cost of taking Vimy Ridge.

After the first day, the Germans regrouped and stiffened their resistance. There were additional gains over the next five days, but with less ease. On August 10, Driver Hesler found himself in Beaufort, which had been taken the day before:

"Enemy planes troubled us a lot here, bombing horse lines nearly every night. Bartlett and I had slept in a grave-like hole we had dug under our stores wagon which was good enough protection while the weather was dry."

War Diary of the 4ᵀᴴ Divisional Ammunition Column for August 10, 1918:
D.A.C. personnel 'dug in' as protection against enemy bombing.

Between August 8 and 13, Currie's four divisions had defeated elements of fifteen German divisions. By the 20th, it had pushed the front back fourteen miles and liberated 27 villages. This was a totally new experience. Instead of a few thousand yards of useless mud littered with corpses, the Canadian troops could measure their efforts in terms of miles of farmland and live civilians. A penchant for mobility and individual initiatives which had always been rooted in Canadian tactics finally got free rein. This was supported by the proficiency of the artillery, engineers and intelligence service, where Borden, for one, considered the Canadians pre-eminent. Brutinel's Mobile Machine Gun Brigade, previously successful in avoiding disasters in a defensive mode, had become a major tactical advantage on the attack and served as a model for the Allied forces as a whole.

Ironically, in their push towards Germany in 1918, the Allies were deprived of one advantage which they were to enjoy in 1944-45: air superiority. There was scarcely a day during those last one hundred on which the Canadian forces did not come under attack from the air.

On August 22, Currie met up with his former Corps Commander, General Byng, who now commanded the British Third Army. Byng's forces had been probing the line north of the Canadian positions for over a year. In November 1917, they had nearly reached the strategically important city of Cambrai, but had been driven back. Byng, perhaps more than any other British general, was able to measure Currie's success at Amiens. He told Currie that the Canadian performance at Amiens was "the finest operation of the war"[12].

Although Foch wanted to press the Amiens offensive forward, Currie sensed that there would be better opportunities for advance elsewhere. He recommended that the gains in front of Amiens be consolidated, that the Canadian Corps be pulled out of the line to rest, and that it be redeployed for a new surprise assault near Arras. Haig, for once, agreed, and sold the idea to Foch. On August 20, the Canadians began to move out of the line and to move northward. The journey was not uneventful:

> "The 4th Division sector was taken over by the French and the tour of the Canadian Corps in the Somme area was completed. On Saturday, August 24th, we abandoned this camp at 9 P.M. and moved towards the north. On the road towards Le Quesnel we fell in behind other units moving out and the line was spotted by German planes which bombed and machine gunned the moving stream of wagons. Our section escaped unhurt but severe damage was done to units ahead of us. We crossed the River Luce and camped at Aubertcourt at 1 A.M. on the 25th. A short but exciting trip."

> WAR DIARY OF THE 4ᵀᴴ DIVISIONAL AMMUNITION COLUMN FOR
> AUGUST 24, 1918:
> Infantry crossing in front delayed movement. Enemy 'plane dropped
> bombs, apparently aimed at infantry. Two bombs fell near D.A.C. 3 men
> killed 10 wounded, 7 animals killed 5 wounded in No. 1 Section.

Meanwhile, on August 10, a badly shaken Ludendorf reported
on the Amiens disaster to Kaiser Wilhelm, who at last concluded the
Germans were at the end of their rope and that the "war must be
terminated". Four days later, the Kaiser ordered peace negotiations to be
opened up through the good offices of a neutral party, and the bombing
of Paris and London was called off. Ludendorf attempted to plod on,
and the killing on the ground went on unabated until the very end.

Almost immediately upon their arrival at Arras, the Canadian
Corps embarked on a series of offensives that drove through the
Hindenberg Line and brought them to Cambrai, the city which had
eluded capture by Byng's Third Army the previous year. Cambrai was a
major distribution centre, supporting much of the German operations
in the entire northern sector of the Front. Its approaches were amongst
the strongest defensive positions in the German line. If Cambrai could
be captured, it was anticipated that the Germans would be forced into
a massive withdrawal from France and Belgium.

From August 26 to October 11, the Canadian Corps advanced a
further 23 miles in a series of exhausting battles which, like Amiens,
were characterized by a mobility not earlier experienced in the war,
but with fighting of relentless intensity. There were nearly 32,000
Canadian casualties. They seem to have been bearable, if only because
of a sense that the war was being won at long last. Although still
capable of putting up punishing resistance, the German army was
being hammered. The delicate balance had swung. Exhausted, forlorn
and with their families at home near starvation from the effects of the
British naval blockade, German soldiers no longer fought to win. They
fought only to survive.

The first of these costly engagements was the Battle of the Scarpe,
August 26-30. Knowing that the Canadians had entered the line near
Arras, the Germans withdrew from the area of Neuville-Vitasse and
concentrated their strength along the Fresnes-Rouvroy defence system,

the first of three fall-back positions before the Hindenberg Line. This first line of defence was broken in three days of fighting in which the 2nd and 3rd Divisions suffered nearly 6,000 casualties.

All of the officers of the 22nd Battalion were killed or wounded in this endeavour. One of the severely wounded was Major Georges Vanier. Vanier was the senior surviving officer and took over command of the Vandoos on August 27. The same day near Chérisy, he was hit in the chest by a machine gun bullet. While being tended to on a stretcher, a German shell exploded nearby. The stretcher bearer was killed, and Vanier's right leg was shattered by shrapnel. It was his ticket out of the conflict, albeit only until it resumed in 1939. In the meantime, the future governor-general briefly enjoyed more peaceful surroundings in the law firm that Driver Hesler would later deal with in his capacity as Secretary of the Royal Bank of Canada[13].

But Driver Hesler came close to going no further than Chérisy himself. By this time, the Red Baron was dead, and so was much of the old chivalric ideals of aerial combat:

> "One evening while we were here I had to ride out on some duty and did not return until late. I now possessed a shining new white bell tent and while I was unsaddling my white horse near the tent a German bomber came over and scattered his load nearby. My white targets were no doubt too inviting and I was soon under a hail of machine-gun lead. No doubt this was the most "outstanding" horse since the Battle of the Boyne. Fortunately, the horse and I were on the edge of a deep shell-hole so quickly shoving him into it and crouching beside his bulk I passed a few nervous moments until Fritz gave up the rabbit hunt."[14]

WAR DIARY OF THE 4TH DIVISIONAL AMMUNITION COLUMN FOR SEPTEMBER 9, 1918:
Billets for personnel very good, now that tents and infantry shelters have been issued.

The next objective was the Drocourt-Quéant Line, the last major German defence system west of the Canal du Nord and considered to be the backbone of the enemy's resistance. Now it was the turn of the 1st and 4th Divisions. On September 3, the Drocourt-Quéant Line was overrun in what Currie described in his diary as a victory greater than Amiens. The British writer Denis Winter describes Currie's capture of the Drocourt-Quéant positions as the "British Army's single greatest achievement on the Western Front"[15]. In four days, the Canadians took 6,000 German prisoners. In a single day, seven Victoria Crosses were awarded to Canadian soldiers.

The Canadian Artillery were drawn out of the line at this point for a brief period of rest and reorganization. By this time, Driver Hesler had become, in a certain way, indispensable:

> "While we were here I had a bit of a set-to with the Sergeant-major who accused me of adding salt to the bacon delivered to the sergeants' mess. We had heard of a lot of German atrocities but this was one on our side that I was sorry that I had not perpetrated, if I had had the time. I smoothed him over and he accepted my avowals of innocence, probably influenced by the fact that he had no one to take my place and he could not demote me because I was as low in rank as I could be."

CANAL DU NORD, 27 SEPTEMBER 1918
AN AMMUNITION COLUMN DRIVES THROUGH THE BREACH

The next barrier was the Canal du Nord, an uncompleted oddity of French civil engineering which was partially above ground. Currie concluded that a frontal attack on this heavily fortified facility would be suicidal if undertaken in the swampy area where the canal held water. He devised instead a carefully prepared shift of his forces to the south to the dry portion of the canal. Relying on the rapid redeployment of the artillery, Currie's concentrated forces punched through the earthworks on September 27 and fanned out beyond the canal. The countryside east of the canal and the German positions in front of Cambrai were dominated by high ground known as Bourlon Wood, which sheltered the defending German artillery from view. Bloody hand-to-hand fighting brought about the capture of Bourlon Wood and set the scene for the attack on Cambrai itself.

WAR DIARY OF THE 4TH DIVISIONAL AMMUNITION COLUMN FOR SEPTEMBER 28, 1918:
Extending along the Eastern side, and about 150 yds from the Canal du Nord in this area, a row of tank traps was discovered. The traps consisted of Minenvefers about 6½ inch caliber placed upright in the ground with special fuzes replacing the ordinary Minenverfer fuze. Over the fuzes heavy 4 x 10 inch plank boards were placed, these in turn were covered with some loose earth to render them inconspicuous.

For Ludendorf, the breach of the Canal du Nord was the last straw. On September 28, he broke down completely. With the German Commander-in-Chief incapacitated, more pragmatic German minds were free to pursue the option of peace more vigorously. The fighting raged on regardless.

The rapidity of the Canadian advance placed enormous demands on the artillery. It was no longer a matter of sighting a barrage to land ahead of the infantry: the guns themselves had to keep pace, and ammunition had to be moved over ground that had been in enemy hands an hour or two before. The rapidity of the advance had left Driver Hesler on the outskirts of Quéant, in charge of four wagons and a contingent of walking wounded. The wagons had been stripped of their animals to replace those killed bringing ammunition to the guns for the attack on the Canal. Again, his luck kept him out of harm's way:

"At last on September 30th the section could find time to send horses to bring us back to the fold and we set off through Quéant towards the Canal du Nord. This canal was in unfinished condition when the war began and held no water. Here it was built over low land by high banks which looked like the wall of China. My rescuers told me that they had lined up with their wagons in support of our guns directly behind the infantry that was to clear the canal and as soon as the way was cleared they had advanced through the captured breach in the walls into the open fields towards Bourlon. We had suffered a number of casualties."

It seems to be a custom of warfare that the safekeeping of booty captured by an invading army is a task which befalls the Quartermaster:

"We rejoined the section at a point behind Bourlon Wood. Soon after I arrived I was summoned to the Captain's tent and I went with some forebodings but I knew that he could not demote me. I found that his section marking flag had been lost in the hurried movements and that no one had been able to find a replacement. Would I get busy and get one from Ordnance? Also, would I keep an eye on the German wagon which he had "captured" and see to it that his souvenirs were not lost? I checked the wagon which was full of oddments picked up along the way so far in the Canadian Corps' "Hundred Days" and found that he was even transporting a bath tub, a rather rare item in that part of France at the time.

We had occasional casualties among our animals and with the Captain's souvenir wagon requiring at least two mules or horses we were now always a little short on draught."

> War Diary of the 4ᵗʰ Divisional Ammunition Column for September 30, 1918:
> From commencement of CAMBRAI operations 21-9-18 to date inclusive, dumps operated by this unit have issued approximately 192,573 rounds Field Artillery Ammunition.

The last obstacle to the capture of Cambrai was the Hindenberg Line itself. The Germans attempted to hold on to it with almost fanatical determination. At one point, they managed to force units of the 1st Division to withdraw from their gains. German tanks were deployed against the Canadians. On October 9, Cambrai fell to Currie's forces. Nine battered German divisions and elements of three others were on the run. The speed of the Canadian advance thwarted German plans to destroy the city by fire, although much of it was damaged in that fashion before the city was secured. It was neither the first nor the last in a series of encounters with a brutal practice of destroying the property and means of subsistence of French civilians in areas which the German Army expected never to regain.

This succession of Canadian advances had been undertaken by Canadian units heavily depleted by casualties. Some battalions went into battle most of the time at half strength. The entire campaign was blanketed daily by German artillery shoots and strafed and bombed by German aircraft. No one had any real rest for weeks on end. New troops, many of them conscripts, were slotted into the action practically on the run.

To either flank of the Canadian spearhead, Foch's other armies were making gains all along the Western Front, but less spectacularly.

To the south, the exhausted French and newly-arrived Americans pushed the German lines back between Reims and Verdun. The overwhelming advantage in manpower resulting from the arrival of the Americans provided the Allies with the opportunity of dealing the German Army a death blow, but the opportunity was missed. Chaotic logistical support and what Denis Winter calls "the disastrous military performance of the Americans" under Pershing allowed the German Army to escape. "If a German general had been put in charge of the Americans, he couldn't have created greater confusion if he had tried."[16] Lloyd George and Foch appealed to President Wilson to remove his inept Commander, but Pershing stayed on. The virtual paralysis of a million-man army led some Allied leaders to despair of finishing the war in 1918. There were fears that the Allied armies would suffer the same fate as had befallen the Germans during their grand offensives of August 1914 and March 1918.

In the North, Messines Ridge and Passchendaele Ridge were recaptured on September 28 by the British and Belgians, but their advance was slowed by the inability of the British forces to adapt to the new mobility of the conflict. At long last, the resilient Belgians were regaining parts of their homeland. The Belgians had endured four years of deprivation and suffering under a brutal German occupation that served as the precursor for worse atrocities a generation later.

While overall the success of Foch's grand offensive was not what it could have been, the war was closer to its end than many thought. The Allied advances, aided by the simultaneous collapse of Germany's Austrian, Bulgarian and Turkish allies, provoked a series of crises in Germany. On October 4, diplomatic notes were sent to President Wilson requesting an armistice. Debate ensued as to whether Wilson's "fourteen points" meant a cease-fire or a surrender. In the meantime, the German forces were ordered to stiffen their resistance as a means of winning the debate.

> WAR DIARY OF THE 4ᵀᴴ DIVISIONAL AMMUNITION COLUMN FOR
> OCTOBER 17, 1918:
> Records show the unit to have been singularly fortunate in regard to Battle casualties. Only 5 having been killed and 38 wounded from April 1ˢᵗ to October 6ᵗʰ 1918.

The capture of Cambrai was not the end of it for the Canadians. The last stop would be Mons, a city forty miles further east. In between lay the Sensée Canal and the city of Valenciennes:

> "On Sunday, October 13th, we left Chérisy and moved forward five or six miles to a camp behind a wood between Récourt and Lécluse in preparation for an attack on the Sensée Canal. We remained here nearly a week and had a few shells and bombs thrown at us. While here our supplies of winter underclothing and

long leather boots were issued. When we left here on Sunday, October 20th we began to move more rapidly. We crossed the low lands of the Sensée River at Lécluse and then went on to the Sensée Canal which had been crossed by the 4th Division infantry on the 18th. This was my first crossing on a pontoon bridge and while I had some trouble with my horse I was amused by the antics of the mules when they felt the bridge bobbing under their feet."

The Canadian advance at this point was mainly an effort to keep up with the German retreat. Pockets of German resistance still had to be dealt with, and the Canadians were continuously harassed by German artillery and aircraft. In addition to the demands on mobility, another logistical problem had to be handled for the first time: thousands of starving civilians, stripped of their food, crops and livestock by the retreating Germans.

DENAIN, OCTOBER 27, 1918
GENERAL CURRIE, THE PRINCE OF WALES, GENERAL MORRISON (COMMANDER OF THE CANADIAN ARTILLERY) AND GENERAL WATSON (COMMANDER OF THE 4TH* DIVISION)*

> **WAR DIARY OF THE 4ᵀᴴ DIVISIONAL AMMUNITION COLUMN FOR OCTOBER 23, 1918:**
> Many civilians in the village, who were left without food of any description. The majority have not eaten bread for two weeks.

In a single day on October 19, the Corps advanced nearly seven miles, taking nearly forty villages and towns, including the large industrial town of Denain. On October 22, Currie called a halt at the River Escaut, to allow the flanking British forces to catch up. The exhausted Canadian divisions used the pause to rest and prepare for the attack on Valenciennes.

"The next day we moved a few more miles to Oisy, a village behind Valenciennes. It had been captured on the 21st. We had a bad time during the latter part of the week we remained here. Our horse lines were shelled heavily on several occasions with the consequent loss of a number of animals. The villagers were torn between resentment at our making them a target and gratitude for the horse and mule flesh which they were able to salvage after each shelling. On each occasion, as soon as the immediate danger had passed they would rush out of the village to our lines and hack away at the carcasses and fight for the choicest bits. I am sure that a nice piece of mule steak was a great treat to them. One evening at dusk I was issuing rum to some of the men who had been up to the guns when Fritz sent over a couple of shells which overshot the horse lines and came close to my tent which I had not dyed. The three or four of us standing within the tent flattened ourselves on the ground. One of the men, trying to make himself as small as possible was crowding his head into my stomach forcing my behind against the hot oil-drum stove which I had stoked up to take off the evening chill. The smell of singeing cloth convinced us that we had been hit but when the shelling ceased we found that there was no damage except a neat hole about two feet in diameter in the tent where my head had been a few minutes earlier. It was no consolation to us that it was discovered next day that we were camped on the wrong side of the village in plain view of the enemy's observers!"

Valenciennes was heavily defended by the Germans, and its capture posed a particular challenge because of the large civilian population. The challenge was greatest for the artillery, who had the task of supporting the attack with as little damage as possible to the city itself. The fall of Valenciennes on November 2 marked the end of the last Canadian battle in France until Dieppe in 1942.

WAR DIARY OF THE 4TH DIVISIONAL AMMUNITION COLUMN FOR NOVEMBER 7, 1918:

Many civilians entering the town [Valenciennes] from neighbouring villages, bearing their goods & chattels on all manner of improvised vehicles. The city was formally handed over to civil authorities by military authorities at 1100 hours today. The ceremony being held in the Place d'Armes, and amongst those present being H.R.H. The Prince of Wales, Lt-Gen. Currie the Canadian Corps Commandant and numerous other Canadian officers. Infantry and artillery of all units who took part in the occupation were present, the 4th Cdn. Division being predominant.

By this time, Canadian soldiers had had their fill of the hardships which the Germans had inflicted on the French population. In addition to the starvation, Driver Hesler noted one particularly mean-spirited piece of mischief:

"One inhuman spectacle was the straying lunatics who had been let loose from confinement in hospital by the Germans when they retired from the city."

Scenes like these did not predispose the Canadian victors to acts of kindness towards the retreating Germans. One battalion noted with apparent disappointment that Germans were surrendering in such large numbers that there was no alternative but to take them prisoner[17]. What happened to smaller groups or individual German soldiers is a matter for conjecture.

The Canadian advance crossed the Belgian border on November 7. Another 15 miles ahead lay Mons. It was at Mons that the British Expeditionary Force had lost its first battle to the Germans in August of 1914. The war was coming full circle. Currie's forces entered the city with scarcely a fight on November 10. The next day, the war ended. Shortly after 11 a.m., a German officer in charge of a unit facing the Canadians on the outskirts of Mons stood up and fired a signal flare into the air. The German soldiers stood up in turn, shouldered their weapons, and marched off in an orderly fashion in the direction of Germany.

WAR DIARY OF THE 4ᵀᴴ DIVISIONAL AMMUNITION COLUMN FOR NOVEMBER 11, 1918:
Armistice came into effect at 1100 hours today, the news being very quietly received.

Driver Hesler recorded his remembrance of that day as follows:

"Early in the morning of Monday, November 11th when I went to the orderly office to check up on the nominal roll for my indents I was told, hush, hush, that a message had been received at Column H.Q. stating that the war would end at eleven o'clock that morning. Strangely, it created no emotional effect and the same applied to most of the men who were paraded at eleven o'clock to receive the announcement and also orders to give the animals an extra good grooming. The end of the war had been expected to occur before winter set in but I think most of us hoped that it would end on German soil. I announced that there would be an extra rum issue that evening but practically all chose to attend the cinema. In the last three months they had received lots of rum but never an opportunity of seeing a motion picture. One or two joined me in a quiet drinking party at my billet and we discussed the future."

CHAPTER SEVEN

THE JOURNEY HOME

The terms of the Armistice provided for Allied forces to advance as far as the Rhine and to occupy both sides of the main bridgeheads. The 1st and 2nd Divisions formed the Canadian occupation force and were assigned the area around Bonn. They crossed the German border on December 4, noting the contrast between cheering Belgian civilians and grim German onlookers. By December 13, after marching 250 miles in miserable weather, they crossed the Rhine. As they paraded across the Bonn bridge, they saluted a victorious General Currie.

> WAR DIARY OF THE 4TH DIVISIONAL AMMUNITION COLUMN FOR NOVEMBER 16, 1918:
> The first stage in the move forward to complete the occupation of the German Rhinelands was made today when the column took the road for ELOUGES at 10:00 hours.

Driver Hesler remained with the 4th Division in Belgium:

"On Saturday, November 16th, we started on what we thought would be a long trek to Germany but the 4th Division never got there. Out along the Valenciennes-Mons road there was a steady stream of civilians returning to their homes pushing barrows, pulling carts and carrying babies, wholly concerned with making progress as rapidly as possible."

It was a dreary winter, in a land which had suffered greatly from more than four years of hardship and deprivation:

"We took up quarters at Cuesmes, a coal-mining suburb of Mons. I was billeted in a very clean house on the main street occupied by an old coal-miner, his wife and their son who had been conscripted by the Germans for labour behind the lines and recently returned. Food was still scarce amongst these people and they partook of only one meal after a very light breakfast. That consisted usually of vegetables that were put on the stove about noon and left to cook until the evening when it was a thick mass that had some chance of sticking to their ribs."

At least these conditions were better than the earlier makeshift billets of canvas and corrugated iron that had sheltered Driver Hesler in the field, summer and winter, during most of the previous two and a half years.

During his short stay in liberated Belgium, Driver Hesler witnessed the same scenario which would play out in liberated France in 1944:

"On our first day in the town one of our new neighbours, a woman accused of having lived with the German officers, was taken from her house and in the street was shorn of her hair—a very temporary scarlet letter. During my three weeks here I made several visits to Mons on duty and I was greatly impressed by the broad avenues and huge trees of this city now so famous in British history. There were long lines of men and women waiting to be interrogated as suspected collaborators.

Christmas 1918 was spent on leave in London.

"About December 30th President Wilson was in London on his way to the opening of the Peace Conference and he was given a rousing reception as his carriage went along The Strand. Following in another coach and four were the Prince of Wales and Lloyd George, the latter looking like the cat that had swallowed the canary. Seeing that the world was in such good hands I decided to return to Belgium and I left from Victoria Station at 7.30 A.M. on December 31st, comfortably settled in a first class compartment where the military guard had placed me in return for a half-crown."

Ordnance Unit, Limelette, Belgium, 1919

WAR DIARY OF THE 4TH DIVISIONAL AMMUNITION COLUMN FOR MARCH 22, 1919:
30 Riding, 36 L.D. horses and 50 mules turned over to Belgian Government.

The process of repatriating the men and equipment of the Canadian Corps occupied the first four months of 1919. Early in March, Driver Hesler became Sergeant Hesler. No longer a muleskinner, his duties were clerical, as part of the administrative burden of disbanding an army on foreign soil.

"The Ordnance Corps had set up an establishment a few miles away in a small chateau at Limelette where they were taking in all of the equipment of the 4th Division under the direction of my old friend, W.O. 1, Don Glendon. Early in March he asked me to join his group to compile and maintain records of this equipment so, in agreement with the Quartermaster-Sergeant who had returned to duty, I went off and took up residence in the chateau which was almost bare of furnishings except for army cots. Apart from a number of men who handled the articles as they came in there were about six of us who functioned as the "executive", all of them sergeants except of course Glendon and me. At Don's request I typed out an order and at the first opportunity had a visiting officer sign it, raising me to the rank of sergeant. This was tacked to the office door and taking stripes from the ample stores under my control to sew on my sleeves I became for the first and last time an N.C.O. but without pay for the rank."

The 4th Division was the last of the Canadian Corps divisions to leave the Continent, and Hesler was one of the last three of its members to do so.

"On some of these early Spring mornings 'my groom' would bring 'my horse' to the house and I would go for a ride in the forests and hills of this area. I was probably the only private in the British forces that had a horse and groom. During this period there came to our H.Q. as Adjutant, a Captain T.H. Atkinson, who had gone overseas in a battery with the First Contingent. Through the scuttlebutt it was learned that he had been with the Royal Bank before enlisting and probably no one except himself expected that one day he would be General Manager of the bank.

By the end of April the last of the 4th Division, except our little "executive" group had left for England. I recall listening in on a telephone conversation between

Atkinson and the Staff Captain in which the latter asked whether the Column was ready to move out. Atkinson said that everything was in order except that there was one man missing – a man named Hesler and they did not know where he was. They might have asked the Q.M.S. of our section as I was still receiving my mail through it, but apparently nobody cared. Anyway, the Staff Captain did not as he decided the matter quickly with 'Let the s.o.b. stay here and rot . . .'. He could not have remembered that I was the man who had roused him early in the morning a year before at Noeux-les-Mines."

RMS AQUITANIA, STILL IN HER ANTI-SUBMARINE CAMOUFLAGE IN 1919

On May 18, Sergeant Hesler boarded the liner *Aquitania* at Southampton, and sailed for Halifax. The *Aquitania* was then one of the largest ships afloat. There were 7,000 men crammed onto that ship when it sailed for Canada. Sixty thousand other Canadians never had a chance to make the journey home.

"Befitting my rank I occupied a cabin with several other sergeants instead of taking turns with those of lower rank in occupying hammocks. As nobody seemed to know who I belonged to I received no orders for duty during the voyage as other sergeants did.

After a couple of days in Montreal, where I gathered together some civilian clothes, I set off, still in uniform, for Humberstone where my father and mother who had not seen me since early 1915 welcomed me at the tiny Grand Trunk station with the hope expressed that I would remain with them for some time."

The war which everyone thought was "the war to end all wars" had come to an end. Arthur Currie died in 1933 at the age of fifty-eight. He deserved to be a national hero, but his enemies at home had seen to it that he never would quite be that in his lifetime. The tragedy of Currie was that, quite apart from his success as a military leader, he was never fully recognized for his contribution in saving the lives of the Canadians who were fortunate enough to have him interposed between themselves and the British high command. The lack of government and popular recognition for his efforts must have dogged him for the rest of his life. He was tormented in his later years by the stresses of a libel action he took to vindicate himself in the face of unfounded insinuations by an obscure Ontario newspaper that he had wantonly squandered the lives of Canadian soldiers in the capture of Mons. Worse than all this, in the days just before he died, he appears to have come to the sad and painful conclusion that the horror he had seen would inevitably resume.

Twenty years after Harold Hesler left Europe, another World War began. Six years later, another artilleryman from the Niagara Peninsula, Lt. William C. Hesler, M.C., boarded the very same *Aquitania* at Southampton, and sailed for home, just as his uncle had done before him.

CHRISTMAS CARD FROM ANOTHER NIAGARA ARTILLERYMAN, NOVEMBER 1944
(ONLY THE LAND TRANSPORTATION HAD CHANGED)

CHAPTER EIGHT

AFTERTHOUGHTS

The Canadian War Memorial at Vimy Ridge

The Canadian memorial at Vimy rises from its broad terrace on the Ridge, an intriguing admixture of monolithic stone architecture and refined allegorical statuary. The largest of these human figures is a female symbol of Canada. She stands at the outer edge of the terrace, her back to the towers. Head bowed, she faces the slope on which Driver Hesler and his mule outran the range of the German shells on April 15, 1917.

The Figure of Canada, mourning her dead

Much has been written about the memorial, the story of its construction and its grand dedication ceremony in 1936. Whatever thoughts and feelings it evokes, it is undeniably a noble tribute to the Canadians who died in the war. At least on the surface, this is no jingoistic salute to the glory of war and empire. There are no flags, no guns, no bronze replicas of fighting men gesturing onward and upward. The sculptured figures express the sadness of loss, but seem more reflective than mourning, perhaps articulating a subtle *Why?*.

Harold Hesler returned to Vimy Ridge in the summer of 1938, during a road trip through northern France and Belgium. One would assume that he viewed the memorial with pride and awe, if not also a sense of gratitude. But the assumption would be wrong. He saw in the monument the same human folly that had driven the war itself. Beneath the surface tribute to the dead, he saw the self-aggrandizement of the generals, the vicarious hero-playing of the politicians, and the complicity of other opinion leaders in Canadian society. One has to wonder how many veterans really didn't want any reminder of the war at all.

> "My disapproval may be expressed in the words of another: 'Admitting the greatness of the event which the monument is there to perpetuate, the latter seems unnecessarily huge, and the thought is impressed upon one—how needless to attempt to equal an achievement by means of a memorial comparable in size?' I am sure that the Canadians who lie in the many beautiful cemeteries along this line believe that they are the true memorial and that the huge pile of granite costing millions is ostentatious."

In fact, while Canadian politicians wanted their British counterparts to take due note of Canada's contribution, and to memorialize it for tourists visiting one of the least attractive regions of France, they had no interest in letting their constituents grasp the true extent of the sacrifice. The price paid had far exceeded the value of anything gained. In a normal person, any impulse to make a proud boast in terms of lives lost would have been stifled by overwhelming feelings of guilt, if not disgust.

This may be the explanation for our expurgated collective memory of the war. If a natural disaster of equal magnitude had befallen the country in those years, we would have a much clearer picture today of just how bad it was. Public knowledge of the war as an event in Canadian history has actually increased in recent years, but the image of the reality has been dim from the very beginning. People may tell tall tales about how they survived a flood or a forest fire, but the survivors of World War I, like Driver Hesler, rarely chose to start a conversation on the topic. The oral history which has been passed down to later generations is hushed. The photographic record is sparse, highly censored and of poor quality. Official policy saw to it that, with few exceptions, the dead were never repatriated. The tens of thousands of grave markers are on view for only those who are prepared to make the pilgrimage to Europe. The other physical markers in Canada are symbolic, not graphic. They consist mainly of quiet epitaphs in town squares, and plaques or regimental flags on display, rather incongruously, in churches. In *Death So Noble*, Jonathan Vance has written a remarkable account of how our collective memory of the tragedy underwent a mythical reconstruction, with the defence of civilization and Christianity cloaking—even sanctifying— the ugly and painful reality of the sacrifice[1]. It may have been a visceral reaction to this guilty glorification that at least partially explains why, 20 years on, Harold Hesler saw through the tokenism of the Vimy Memorial.

Today, Canada has a population of about 34 million. In 1914-1918, the people of Canada and Newfoundland numbered around 8 million. 625,000 enlisted in the war effort or were drafted, representing a large percentage of the productive population. All proportions kept, what kind of world would we be living in today if there had to be 2,500,000 Canadians in the armed forces, instead of the current 67,000? How would we feel if we were forced into a war in which one out of every ten was killed and one out of every four was wounded? That, in relative terms, is the scope of the disaster which befell an earlier generation of Canadians. After such losses, how long would it take us to return to where we were before it all happened? If we reflect on this, we can begin to have an idea of the cost of the war on the Canadians who survived it.

The horrors of the 1914-1918 conflagration were such that, when it was over, some optimistic people were convinced that the civilized world would never allow war to break out again. However, within less than a generation, what had been called the *Great War* had to be renamed *World War One*. The "War to end all wars" had become merely the precursor to an even greater conflict. *World War Two* left more room for cynics than for optimists, and as soon as *it* was over, the phrase "*World War Three*" was coined in anticipation of the inevitable next round.

The realities of mutually assured thermonuclear destruction have, for more than half a century, dissuaded the major powers from going at *each other* again, but none of them has avoided warfare altogether. In a sense, *World War Three* has been raging for years in a series of smaller-scale, but equally intense conflicts all over the globe. Grand attempts at a new international order have failed dismally to prevent armed territorial aggression, genocide and political and religious pogroms.

Driver Hesler was born and raised in a southern Ontario society that had never experienced real war. The oral history on either side of his family contained only anecdotes of armed conflict[2]. How in the 1870s the militia fought off Fenian raiders from the U.S. while his father's family fled westwards in a wagon to the garrison at Port Colborne. How de Salaberry's handful of Québécois skirmishers beat back 5,000 American invaders near Valleyfield in 1813. Laura Secord leading her beautiful cow through the American pickets. Joseph Brant, Rogers' Rangers and Tecumseh.

It was from this innocence of the reality of warfare that Harold Hesler stepped into the recruiting station in Winnipeg in January 1916. Once in, there was no way out. A very succinct, but complete analysis of why men like him found themselves entrapped in the horrors of World War One is contained in a single sentence in a book by a front-line war correspondent:

> *"Loyalty to their own side, discipline, with the death penalty behind it, spell-words of old tradition, obedience to the laws of war, or to the caste which ruled them, all the moral and spiritual propaganda handed out by pastors, newspapers, generals, staff officers, old men at home, exalted women, female furies, a deep and simple love for England, and Germany, pride of manhood, fear of cowardice—a thousand complexities of thought and sentiment prevented men, on both sides, from breaking the net of fate in which they were entangled, and revolting against that mutual, unceasing massacre, by a rising from the trenches with a shout of, "We're all fools! . . . Let's all go home!"'*[3]

Canada at the beginning of the 20th century was an extremely ordered society. In 1914, loyalty to the British Crown was not just a social requirement: along with serving the Creator, it was, for many people, one of the fundamental guiding influences of daily life. The resulting social pressures for enlistment in the early part of the war were so strong that, in most parts of English Canada, there was scarcely any need for coercion of any sort. It is clear from the first chapter of *War Interlude* that these social pressures, rather than any grander aspirations, were what propelled Driver Hesler through the door. *Why* he got entangled is the easy question. This book has attempted to answer the question, *"What was it like?"*. The etching which appears on the cover of this book was drawn from a New York Times article whose title poses an even more difficult one: *"Was it worth it?"*

It is gratuitous and facile to write off Canada's share of the human cost of the war to "nation building". That is surely not the answer to the question. The search for a Canadian identity is not over yet if we have to look in places like Vimy Ridge to find it. Looking beyond the hackneyed symbols it left us with, the war probably did more to retard Canada's development as a nation than to promote it. Every country in Europe was crippled by the war, and destruction of property made up only a small part of the loss. By the same logic, a young country, even one which suffered no physical damage, is not made stronger when a significant percentage of its productive population—including a disproportionate number of those with higher education—are killed or maimed. Nor is the unity of a country encouraged when conscription for service in a foreign conflict causes a profound rift along language lines which is still being exploited today by those who would break up the country. In attempting to answer the question of whether the things Canadian soldiers did in the war were worth the cost, the assessment should examine what they accomplished on the ground, without attempting to measure ethereal things like nationalistic sentiment, which is a commodity of dubious value anyway.

Perhaps the right question to ask is whether Canada's participation in the war made any real difference in the outcome. But "outcome" is a term which, in the peculiar circumstances of the first world war, is fraught with its own controversies.

Early in this book the point was made that, in contrast with the second world war, it is hard to characterize the first one as a struggle between good and evil. If, with the passage of time, the outcome came to be described as an Allied victory over the Central Powers, it is not self-evident that it was the good guys who won, particularly since the stupidity of the Allies was as much to blame for starting the war as the stupidity of the other guys. Moreover, if victory it was, it was pyrrhic, because it helped create the circumstances which spawned the horrors that began to simmer a decade or so later. For this reason, perhaps the only yardstick by which to justly measure anyone's efforts in the first world war is the extent to which they shortened it.

Whatever can be said for the attrition inflicted on the Germans at Vimy or during the final round at Passchendaele, it is clear that the end of the war was hastened by the success of the Canadian spearhead in the assaults of the last hundred days. During that period, 70,000 Canadian troops accomplished more in terms of territorial gains, towns and villages liberated, and German soldiers and weapons captured than 500,000 Americans were able to account for. This is not to take anything away from the Americans, without whose ballast the Allied ship might have floundered in March and April, 1918. But, even after the failure of the German offensive, practically everyone, from muleskinner to Prime Minister, never thought that the war would be over by the end of the year.

In a scathing criticism of his country's military and political leaders, the British author of *Haig's Command* describes the Canadian Corps as by far the most effective fighting unit on the Allied side and Currie as the most successful Allied general of the war[4]. Denis Winter attributes the Canadian success to a number of factors. Among these are the *esprit de corps* created first by Byng and then Currie, the ability of Currie to pick and motivate competent senior officers, a preoccupation with careful training, and a willingness to innovate. In this latter respect, Winter finds that the only army equal to the Canadians was the Germans'[5]. In contrast, he portrays the British forces as badly-led, poorly trained, unmotivated and stuck in their ways.

So, in the context of a people who had no real choice in the matter, the sacrifices made by Canadians were worth it. They made a difference. Under less resourceful and determined leadership, there might very well have been just as many Canadian casualties, but far less, or even nothing, to show for it in terms of bringing the war to its end.

The significance of the Canadian contribution was effectively side-stepped for much of the century. Daniel Dancocks notes that the Canadian effort at Passchendaele got short shrift in the war literature, and suggests that this is due to the fact that the success of Currie's Canadians tended to undermine the criticism levelled at the British High Command for the disastrous results of the three preceding months. A good example which supports Dancock's theory is the single sentence which is devoted to the Canadian achievement at Passchendaele in Martin Gilbert's 550-page *First World War*, published in 1994.

Another reason for the lack of regard for this and other Canadian efforts in the official records of the war may lie in the attitude of British military report writers towards upstart colonials and their senior officers drawn from the part-time militia. Bernard Montgomery, then a junior British staff officer who would rise to the rank of Field Marshal during World War II, wrote in November 1917 that: "The Canadians are a queer crowd; they seem to think they are the best troops in France and that we get them to do our most difficult jobs"[6]. Press reports of the fighting were strictly controlled, and it was a policy of the British authorities to view Canadian or other Dominion units as nothing more than branches of the British military. This continued even after the Canadian and Australian armies had achieved their own separate identities in the minds of anyone aware of what was really happening in the war. When Currie finally recaptured the Belgian city first lost by the British early in the war, the headlines in the London press proclaimed: "*BRITISH TAKE MONS. CROWNING TRIUMPH IN LAST HOURS OF THE WAR*".

This failure to acknowledge Canadian achievements in the official reports and press communiqués then influenced the content of the post-war literature. The German and French Generals gave more credit to the Canadians than their British counterparts did in their memoirs. It would have outraged a lot of British Regular Army officers had they known that in the summer of 1918, fearing the war would continue into the following year, Lloyd George had begun to consider Currie, a former school teacher from Victoria B.C., as one of the few likely candidates to succeed Haig as commander-in-chief of the British Army[7].

Even the common soldier was fair game for condescension, as Driver Hesler found out on his first leave to London:

> "During this visit I saw for the first time the changing of the guard at Buckingham Palace where we were cautioned by a burly Sergeant-Major in terms which often caused fistic combat between the British and Canadian troops. Here we had to submit to 'mind now, you bloody colonials to salute when the colours pass'."

The British Empire ceased to exist more than half a century ago. Since then, imperial conflicts of a different sort have continued to arise, as they have throughout history. Perhaps because of the lessons learned during the four years covered by this book, Canada has, for the most part, declined to be anyone's lackey in those contests.

ILLUSTRATIONS AND CREDITS

H. G. Hesler

Photo: Driver Harold Hesler, No. 3 Section, 3rd Divisional Ammunition Column

Map of the Eastern and Western fronts from a German propaganda booklet "liberated" by Driver Hesler at Valenciennes, 1918

Technical drawing of an 18-pounder shrapnel shell from the field manual carried by Driver Hesler

Photo: A break during boot camp at Witley, Surrey, June 1916

Canadian Army Christmas card, 1917

Photo: Ordnance Unit, Limelette, 1919

Canadian Army Christmas card, 1944

William Hesler

Photo: the figure of Canada, mourning her dead

Kerr Eby

Cover etching: "Rough going", 1919

A. W. Elson & Co.

Portrait photo: Arthur Currie, 1919

Records and Archives Canada

Photo: Mule team drawing ammunition on the Inner Circle near Vimy

Photo: Pack horses transporting ammunition to the 20th Battery, April 1917

Photo: Wounded Canadians at Passchendaele

Photo: Nursing sisters voting, 1917

Photo: Denain, October 27, 1918

Department of Veterans' Affairs

Photo: Canadian War Memorial at Vimy Ridge

Imperial War Museum

Photo: Artillerymen at Orville, October 1916

Photo: Improvised slings for the mud of the Somme

Photo: Ammunition Column on the Somme, October 1916

Photo: Haig makes a point with Lloyd George, December 1916

Photo: One of Diver Hesler's Mules

Photo: Australian muleskinners at work near Passchendaele, 1917

Photo: German prisoners being marched into Ypres, September 1917

Photo: Pack mules pass by a wrecked artillery limber near Ypres, July 1917

Photo: Canal du Nord, September 27, 1918

Photo: RMS Aquitania, 1919

BIBLIOGRAPHY

Canadian authors

Aitken, Max (Lord Beaverbrook), *Canada in Flanders,* Hodder and Stoughton, London 1917.

Aitken, Max (Lord Beaverbrook), *Politicians and the War 1914-1916*, Thornton Butterworth, London 1928.

Aitken, Max (Lord Beaverbrook), *Men and Power 1917-1918*, Hutchinson, London 1957.

Bennett, Capt. S.G., *The 4th Canadian Mounted Rifles 1914-1919,* Murray Printing, Toronto 1926.

Berton, Pierre, *Vimy*, McClelland and Stewart, Toronto 1986.

Bird, Will R., *Thirteen Years After: The Story of the Old Front Revisited*, MacClean, Toronto 1932.

Black, Ernest G., *I Want One Volunteer*, Ryerson, Toronto, 1965.

Borden, Robert Laird, *His Memoirs,* MacMillan, Toronto 1938.

Bruce, Col. Herbert A., *Politics and the C.A.M.C.*, William Briggs, Toronto 1919.

Canadian Field Comforts Commission, *With the First Canadian Contingent*, Hodder & Stoughton, Toronto, 1915.

Christie, N. M., *Slaughter in the Mud: The Canadians at Passchendaele 1917*, CEF Books 1998.

Clark, H. D., *Extracts from the War Diary and Official Records of the Second Canadian Divisional Ammunition Column*, St. John 1921.

Cooke, O. A., *The Canadian Military Experience 1867-1995: A Bibliography*, Ottawa 1997.

Dancocks, Daniel G., *Legacy of Valour: The Canadians at Passchendaele*, Hurtig, Edmonton 1986.

Dancocks, Daniel G., *Welcome to Flanders Fields: The First Canadian Battle of the Great War: Ypres, 1915*, McClelland and Stewart, Toronto 1988.

Dancocks, Daniel G., *Gallant Canadians: The Story of the Tenth Canadian Infantry Battalion*, Calgary 1990.

Dawson, Coningsby, *Carry On: Letters in War-Time*, John Lane, New York 1917.

Douglas, Lt. J. Harvey, *Captured: Sixteen Months as a Prisoner of War*, McClelland, Toronto 1918.

Duguid, Col. A. Fortescue, *The Canadian Forces in The Great War 1914-1919*, King's Printer, Ottawa 1938.

Duncan-Clark, Plewman and Wallace, *Pictorial History of the Great War*, Nichols, Toronto 1919.

Fetherstonhaugh, R.C., *The 13th Battalion Royal Highlanders of Canada 1914-1919*, Gazette Printing, Montreal 1925.

Fetherstonhaugh, R.C., *The Royal Montreal Regiment, 14th Battalion, C.E.F. 1914-1925*, Gazette Printing, Montreal 1927.

Fetherstonhaugh, R.C., *The Royal Canadian Regiment 1883-1933*, Gazette Printing, Montreal 1936.

Fetherstonhaugh, R.C., *The 24th Battalion, C.E.F., Victoria Rifles of Canada 1914-1919*, Gazette Printing, Montreal 1930.

Goodspeed, D.J., *The Road Past Vimy: The Canadian Corps 1914-1918*, Macmillan, Toronto 1969.

Goodspeed, D.J., *Ludendorf: Genius of World War I*, Macmillan, Toronto 1966.

Hodder-Williams, Ralph, *Princess Patricia's Canadian Light Infantry 1914-1919*, Hodder and Stoughton, London 1923.

Hyatt, A.M.J., *General Sir Arthur Currie: A Military Biography*, University of Toronto Press, Toronto 1987.

Johnston, James Robert, *Riding into War: The Memoir of a Horse Transport Driver, 1916-1919*, Goose Lane, Fredericton 2004.

Keshen, Jeffrey A., *Propaganda and Censorship During Canada's Great War*, University of Alberta Press, 1996.

Livesay, J.F.B., *Canada's Hundred Days*, Thomas Allen, Toronto 1919.

Macfarlane, David, *The Danger Tree*, Toronto 1991.

Macksey, Major Kenneth, *The Shadow of Vimy Ridge*, Ryerson Toronto 1965.

MacMillan, Margaret, *Paris 1919*, Random House, New York 2001.

MacPhail, Andrew, *Official History of the Canadian Forces in the Great War: The Medical Services*, Ottawa 1925.

Mathieson, William D., *My Grandfather's War*, Macmillan, Toronto 1981.

McCrae, John, *In Flanders Fields*, William Briggs, Toronto 1919.

McWilliams, James and R. James Steel, *Amiens: Dawn of Victory*, Dundurn, Toronto 2001.

Morton, Desmond, *A Military History of Canada*, Hurtig, Edmonton, 1985.

Morton, Desmond, *When Your Number's Up: The Canadian Soldier in the First World War*, Random House 1993.

Morton, Desmond and J. L. Granatstein, *Marching to Armageddon: Canadians and the Great War 1914-1919*, Dennys 1989.

Nicholson, Col. G.W.L., *Canadian Expeditionary Force 1914-1919*, Queen's Printer, Ottawa 1962.

Nicholson, Col. G.W.L., *The Gunners of Canada, Vol. I*, Beauceville 1967.

O'Shea, Stephen, *Back to the Front, An Accidental Historian Walks the Trenches of World War I*, Douglas & McIntyre, Toronto 1996.

Pearson, Lester B., *Memoirs*, University of Toronto Press, Toronto 1972.

Rawling, Bill, *Surviving Trench Warfare: Technology and the Canadian Corps, 1914-1918*, University of Toronto Press, Toronto, 1992.

Roberts, Maj. Charles G.D., *Canada in Flanders*, Hodder and Stoughton, London 1918.

Roy, Reginald H., (ed.), *The Journal of Private Fraser 1914-1918*, CEF Books 1998.

Scott, Canon Frederick George, *The Great War as I Saw It*, Goodchild, Toronto 1922.

Sheldon-Williams, Inglis and Ralf Frederic Lardy *The Canadian Front in France and Flanders*, Black, London 1920.

Speaight, Robert, *Vanier*, Collins, Toronto 1970.

Stanley, George F.G., *Canada's Soldiers 1604-1954*, Macmillan, Toronto 1954.

Tamblyn, Lt. Col. D. S., *The Horse in War,* Jackson Press, Kingston.

Topp, Lt. Col. C. Beresford, *The 42nd Battalion, C.E.F. Royal Highlanders of Canada*, Gazette Printing Co., Montreal 1931.

Urquhart, Lt. Col. H.M., *The History of the 16th Battalion (The Canadian Scottish) in the Great War, 1914-1919*, Macmillan, Toronto 1932.

Urquhart, Lt. Col. H.M., *Arthur Currie*, Dent, Toronto 1950.

Vance, Jonathan F., *Death So Noble: Memory, Meaning and the First World War*, UBC Press, Vancouver 1997.

Wells, Lieut. Clifford Almon, *From Montreal to Vimy Ridge and Beyond*, McClelland, Toronto 1917.

Williams, Jeffery, *Princess Patricia's Canadian Light Infantry*, Cooper, London 1972.

Worthington, Larry, *Amid the Guns Below: The Story of the Canadian Corps (1914-1919)*, McClelland and Stewart, Toronto 1965.

The Call to Arms: Montreal's Role of Honour: European War, 1914, Southam Press, Montreal 1914

The Story of the Sixty-Sixth C.F.A., Edinburgh 1919.

Report of the Ministry, Overseas Military Forces of Canada 1918, London 1919.

Various authors, *Canada in the Great War*, Toronto, 1921

Army handbooks

Handbook of the 18-pr. Q.F. Gun, 1914.

Field Artillery Training, 1914.

Field Service Pocket Book, 1914.

British Authors

Barnes, B.S., *This Righteous War*, Netherwood, 1990.

Barnett, Correlli, *The Great War*, G.P. Putnam's Sons, New York 1979.

Bickersteth, John, ed., *The Bickersteth Diaries, 1914-1918*, Vanwell, 1996.

Blunden, Edmund, *Undertones of War*, Doubleday, London 1929.

Boraston, J. H. (ed.), *Sir Douglas Haig's Despatches*, Dent, London 1920.

Brophy, John, *The Five Years*, Barker, London 1936.

Buchan, John, *Episodes of the Great War*, Thomas Nelson, Toronto 1936.

Cable, Boyd, (Ernest Andrew Ewart) *Action Front*, McClelland, Toronto, 1916.

Cable, Boyd, (Ernest Andrew Ewart) *Between The Lines*, E.P. Dutton, New York 1915.

Callwell, Maj.-Gen. Sir C.E., *Field-Marshall Sir Henry Wilson*, Cassel, London 1927.

Cameron, James, *1914*, Cassell, London,1959.

Chapman, Guy (ed.), *Vain Glory*, Cassell, London 1937.

Churchill, Winston S., *The World Crisis*, Macmillan, Toronto 1931.

Cooper, Duff, *Haig*, Macmillan, Toronto 1935.

Cooper, Tilly, *Animals in War*, Imperial War Museum, 1983

Crozier, Brig.-Gen. F.P., *The Men I Killed*, Michael Joseph, London 1937.

Ellis, John, *Eye-Deep in Hell: Trench Warfare in World War I*, Pantheon, New York 1976.

Falls, Cyril, *War Books: A Critical Guide*, Davies, London, 1930.

Viscount French of Ypres, Field-Marshal, *1914*, Constable, London 1919.

Fraser, David, ed., *In Good Company, The First World War Letters and Diaries of The Hon. William Fraser, Gordon Highlanders*, Russell Publishing, Salisbury 1990.

Gibbs, Philip, *Now It Can Be Told*, Harper, New York 1920.

Gibbs, Philip, *The Battles of the Somme*, Doran, New York 1917.

Gilbert, Martin, *First World War*, Stoddart, London 1994.

Giles, John, *Flanders Then and Now*, London 1987.

Gliddon, Gerald *The Battle of the Somme, A Topographical History*, Sutton Publishing, 1994.

Graves, Robert, *Good-bye to All That*, Cape, London 1929.

Hart, Liddell, *The War in Outline 1914-1918*, Faber, London 1936.

Haythornwaite, Philip J., *A Photohistory of World War One*, Arms and Armour Press, London 1994.

Holmes, Richard, *Firing Line*, Penguin 1985.

Horne, Alistair, *The Price of Glory: Verdun 1916*, Penguin 1993.

Horne and Austin (ed.), *Source Records of the Great War*, 1923.

Keegan, John, *The Face of Battle*, Penguin, London 1978.

Laffin, John, *Panorama of the Western Front*, Grange Books, London 1994.

Lloyd George, David, *War Memories*, Ivor Nicholson, London 1933.

Macdonald, Lyn, *Voices and Images of the Great War*, Michael Joseph, London, 1988.

Macdonald, Lyn, *They Called it Passchendaele*, Penguin, London, 1993.

Masefield, John, *The Old Front Line*, Macmillan, New York 1917.

Maze, Paul, *A Frenchman in Khaki*, Heinemann, London 1934.

McCarthy, Chris, *The Somme, The Day-By-Day Account*, Greenwich Editions, London 1993

Mottram, R.H., *Journey to the Western Front: Twenty Years After*, Bell, London 1936

Newman & Evans (ed.), *Anthology of Armageddon*, Archer, London 1935

The Earl of Oxford and Asquith, *Memories and Reflections: 1952-1927*, Little, Brown, Boston 1928.

Robertson, Field-Marshal Sir William, *From Private to Field-Marshal*, Constable, London 1921.

Sassoon, Siegfried, *Memoirs of an Infantry Officer*, Faber & Faber, London 1930.

Strachan, Hew, *The First World War*, Vol. 1, Oxford 2001.

Swinton, Sir Ernest (ed.), *Twenty Years After*, Newnes, London 1937.

Taylor, A. J. P., *The First World War: an Illustrated History*, London 1963.

Warner, Philip, *World War One: A Chronological Narrative*, Arms and Armour Press, London 1995.

Winter, Denis, *Haig's Command*, Viking, London 1991.

Winter, Denis, *Death's Men: Soldiers of the Great War*, Penguin, London 1979.

Wolff, Leon, *In Flanders Fields*, Penguin, London 1979

German authors

Binding, Rudolf (trans.), *A Fatalist at War*, Allen & Unwin, London 1929.

von Ludendorf, Erich (trans.), *Ludendorf's Own Story*, Harper, New York 1919.

Ludwig, Emil, *July '14*, Putnam, New York 1929.

Zweig, Arnold (trans.), *The Case of Sergeant Grischa*, Viking, New York 1928.

Zweig, Arnold (trans.), *Education Before Verdun*, Viking, New York 1936.

French authors

Joffre, Marshal Joseph, *Memoirs*, Geoffrey Bles, London 1932.

Romains, Jules, *Verdun: The Prelude; The Battle*, Alfed Knopf, New York 1939.

American authors

Allen, Hervey, *Toward the Flame*, Grosset & Dunlap, New York 1926.

Davis, Richard Harding, *With the Allies*, Scribner, New York 1914.

Johnson, Douglas W., *Battlefields of the World War*, New York 1921.

Lafore, Laurence, *The Long Fuse: An Interpretation of the Origins of World War I*, Lippincott, Philadelphia, 1971.

Millis, Walter, *Road to War: America 1914-1917*, Houghton Mifflin, Boston 1935.

Palmer, R.R., *A History of the Modern World*, Knopf, New York 1960.

Pershing, General John J., *My Experiences in the World War*, Hodder and Stoughton, London 1931.

Stallings, Laurence (ed.), *The First World War: A Photographic History*, Simon and Schuster, New York 1933.

Tuchman, Barbara W., *The Guns of August*, Macmillan, New York 1962.

END NOTES

Introduction

1. These official records, which became accessible on line only recently, confirm the accuracy of the many places and dates recorded by Harold Hesler in *War Interlude.*

2. The full quote reads: *"But in all the filth and stupidities of that experience I saw courage, fortitude, sacrifice, self-abnegation, generosity yes, and tenderness, compassion and idealism of a quality and an amount that I have not seen since".*

Chapter One

1. In military jargon, the term "casualty" includes those killed, wounded, missing in action and taken prisoner. In a war of attrition, the result, from the perspective of those inflicting the casualty, was practically the same in each case. (In the circumstances of World War I, "missing in action" almost always meant "killed").

2. John Brophy, *The Five Years*, Barker, London 1936, p. 13.

3. *Almanac illustré de la Gazette des Ardennes pour 1918*, distributed mainly to French prisoners of war.

4. Brophy, p. 269.

5. Keegan, *The Face of Battle*, Penguin, London 1978, p. 217.

6. Keegan, p. 269.

7. After he retired from the Royal Bank, H.G. Hesler became a director of Enamel and Heating Products Limited. During World War I, most of the production of the company's stove and bathtub factory in Sackville, New Brunswick consisted of artillery shells of the sort which Driver Hesler hauled to the front line.

Chapter Two

1. One of the soldiers in the German Army who spent nearly the entire war in this area and yet survived had earlier been rejected on medical grounds by the army of his native Austria. His name was Adolph Hitler.

2. Captain F.A.C. Scrimger, who received a Victoria Cross for his efforts two days later carrying Canadian wounded from under enemy fire as German artillery and infantry attempted to follow up on the ravages of the gas.

3. Currie was born in Ontario in 1875 and moved to British Columbia in his teens. A some-time school teacher, insurance salesman and land speculator before the War, he was Principal of Montreal's McGill University from 1920 until his death in 1933. In this latter capacity, he appears in the composite photograph of the Commerce graduates of 1926, one of whom was Driver Hesler's future wife, Edith Aimée Gravel.

4. John Ellis, *Eye-Deep in Hell: Trench Warfare in World War I,* Pantheon, New York 1976 (unattributed).

5. The P.P.C.L.I. were originally formed at the outbreak of war on the initiative and with the financing of a Montreal businessman, A. Hamilton Gault. The Regiment landed in France on December 21, 1914 as part of a British brigade.

6. McCrae was previously a physician at Montreal's Royal Victoria Hospital and had taught medicine at McGill University. He died of pneumonia at the Canadian military hospital which he helped run at Boulogne in January, 1918. One of his colleagues there was

Colonel J.M. Elder, who was the grandfather of the paediatrician who attended Driver Hesler's two grandsons.

7. Two or more divisions made up a corps; two or more corps made up an army.

8. Sir George Perley, lumber baron and member of Parliament for Argenteuil for 26 years, whose name adorns the bridge which spans the Ottawa River between Hawkesbury and Grenville.

9. Col. G.W.L. Nicholson, *Canadian Expeditionary Force 1914-1919*, Queen's Printer, Ottawa 1962, p. 128.

10. Ten years later, as Governor-General of Canada, he provoked a constitutional crisis when he refused to dissolve Parliament after a successful vote of non-confidence and invited Arthur Meighen to form a government.

11. Nicholson, p. 150.

12. Lieutenant-General was the rank reserved for the commander of a corps, General for the commander of an army, and Field Marshal for a group of armies.

13. A hunter named Dunstall was gravely injured when the bolt of his Ross rifle blew back into his face on firing. In 1921, the Supreme Court of Canada upheld his damage action against Sir Charles Ross, ruling that a negligent manufacturer could be directly liable to the consumer.

Chapter Three

1. *War Memoirs of David Lloyd George*, London 1934, vol. III, page 1407.

2. Ellis, p. 94 (unattributed).

3. Joseph Chaballe, *Histoire du 22e Bataillon canadien-français, 1914-1919*, Montreal 1952.

4. Larry Worthington, *Amid the Guns Below: The Story of the Canadian Corps (1914-1919)*, McClelland and Stewart, Toronto

1965, p. 23. Larry Worthington wrote one of the two most readable short histories of the Canadian Corps in World War I. The other is Colonel Goodspeed's *The Road Past Vimy*. One would not know it from her first name, but Larry Worthington was the wife of General Frank Worthington, the founder of the Canadian Armoured Corps.

5. Nicholson, p. 191.

6. Nicholson, p. 192.

7. Nicholson, p. 193.

8. Worthington, p. 60.

9. Despatch of December 23, 1916 reproduced in *Sir Douglas Haig's Despatches*, London 1920, p. 52.

10. Brophy, p. 63.

11. Duff Cooper, *Haig*, Macmillan, Toronto 1935, p. 283

12. A.M.J. Hyatt, *General Sir Arthur Currie: A Military Biography*, University of Toronto Press, Toronto 1987, p. 66.

13. Nicholson, p. 534.

14. Denis Winter, *Haig's Command*, Viking, London 1991, p. 148.

15. *War Memoirs of David Lloyd George*, vol. VI, p. 3367.

Chapter Four

1. A division was a self-contained fighting unit made up of about 20,000 soldiers (or rather, "officers and men" in the correct language of the day). These were divided into three infantry brigades, each of four battalions of 1000 infantry, plus supporting artillery, engineers, field hospitals and other back-up.

2. "Moaning Minnie" was the name Canadians used for the *minenwerfer*, the dreaded German heavy mortar shell.

3. The fate of Bang is disclosed later on.

4. General Lipsett was killed one month before the end of the War.

5. The inscription on the Memorial erected on the site reads: *"To the valour of their countrymen in the Great War and in memory of their sixty thousand dead this monument is raised by the people of Canada"*.

6. Canadian Army Historical Section, quoted by Worthington at page 72.

7. The leader of Vichy France who collaborated with the Nazis during World War II.

8. Plus an extra combat allowance of 10 cents a day.

9. Ellis, p. 64.

10. Nicholson, p. 263.

11. Ernest G. Black, Q.C., *I Want One Volunteer,* Toronto 1965, pp 95 and 108. Black was a friend of Driver Hesler's older brother, Norman Hesler.

12. The Imperial War Museum attributes this photo to a mule on the Somme in 1916.

13. Daniel G. Dancocks, *Legacy of Valour: The Canadians at Passchendaele,* Hurtig, Edmonton 1986, p. 94.

14. Desmond Morton, *When Your Number's Up: The Canadian Soldier in the First World War,* Random House 1993, p. 250.

15. Nicholson, p. 291.

16. Nicholson, p. 292.

17. Nicholson, p. 297.

18. Aitken, born in Beaverbrook, New Brunswick, was the London newspaper magnate now better known by his peerage title.

Chapter Five

1. Cooper, Vol. 1, p. 298

2. Robert Laird Borden, *His Memoirs,* Macmillan, Toronto 1938, p. 809.

3. See Chapter Four.

4. Dancocks, p. 66.

5. Dancocks, p. 86.

6. Cooper, Vol. 2, p. 149.

7. Dancocks, p. 121.

8. *Source Records of the Great War*, Vol. 5, p 297. Before the War, Watson was a militia colonel and the managing director of the Quebec City *Chronicle.*

9. Lyn Macdonald, *Voices and Images of the Great War*, Michael Joseph, London, 1988, p. 220.

10. Dancocks, p. 96.

11. Nicholson, p. 314.

12. Lieutenant Edwin Campion Vaughan, quoted by Richard Holmes, *Firing Line*, Penguin 1985, p. 186

13. Sergeant T.T. Shields, quoted by Dancocks at p. 110.

14. *Source Records of the Great War*, Vol. V, p. 301.

15. Morton, *A Military History of Canada*, Hurtig, Edmonton 1985, p. 162.

16. *War Memoirs of David Lloyd George*, London 1934, vol. IV, p. 2110.

17. Taylor, A. J. P., *The First World War: an Illustrated History*, London 1963, p.148

18. Lester B. Pearson, *Memoirs*, University of Toronto Press, Toronto 1972, vol. 1, p. 36.

Chapter Six

1. Minister of Overseas Military Forces of Canada, *Report of the Ministry, 1918*, p. 108.

2. Borden, p. 818.

3. Minister of Overseas Military Forces of Canada, *Report of the Ministry, 1918*, p. 116.

4. Nicholson, p. 381.

5. Borden, pages 809-811.

6. "Tipping the Balance: The Canadian Corps in 1918", in *The Beaver*, Oct.-Nov. 1989.

7. Minister of Overseas Military Forces of Canada, *Report of the Ministry, 1918*, p. 106.

8. Spain being neutral, it reported its encounter with the pandemic, while censorship kept the lid on its impact on the warring populations. One theory of the epidemiologists is that it originated in the British staging camp at Étaples, about 100 km west of the Canadian lines.

9. Borden, page 810.

10. Minister of Overseas Military Forces of Canada, *Report of the Ministry, 1918*, page 184.

11. Ludendorf, Erich von, *Ludendorf's Own Story*, vol. II, p. 326.

12. Nicholson, p. 424.

13. Now known as Ogilvy Renault.

14. The commander of the German fighter wing in this theatre was now a certain Lieut. Hermann Goering.

15. Winter, p. 271.

16. Winter, p. 219.

17. Nicholson, p. 475.

Chapter 8

1. Vance, Jonathan F., *Death So Noble*, UBC Press, 1997.

2. In contrast, the Quebec experience with a brutal invasion in 1759-60 and bitter civil conflict in 1837-38 made for a less benign collective memory of what war really is.

3. Phillip Gibbs, *Realities of War*, quoted by Martin Gilbert at p. 219.

4. Denis Winter, *Haig's Command*, pp. 131 and 270.

5. Winter, p. 132.

6. Dancocks, p. 102.

7. Urquart, pp. 226-7.